NOTHING BETWEEN

NOTHING BETWEEN

A DEVOTIONAL FOR SENIORS

DIANE HARPER

REDEMPTION
PRESS

Published by Redemption Press, PO Box 427, Enumclaw, WA 98022.

All Scripture, unless otherwise indicated, is taken from the *New American Standard Bible*. Copyright 1960, 1962, 1963, 1968, 1971, 1972, 1973, 1975, 1977, The Lockman Foundation, La Habra, CA.

Scripture reference is taken from *New International Version Study Bible*. Copyright 1985 by the Zondervan Corporation.

Quotes are taken from *My Utmost for His Highest* by Oswald Chambers, edited by James Reimann, © 1992 by Oswald Chambers Publication Assn., Ltd., and used by permission of Discovery House Publishers, Grand Rapids MI 49501. All rights reserved.

ISBN 13: 978-1-63232-940-0

Library of Congress Catalog Card Number: 2009904208

To those on the Senior Citizen journey,

Thou wilt make known to me the path of life;
In Thy presence is fullness of joy;
In Thy right hand there are pleasures forever.
(Psalm 16:11)

A FEW WORDS
ABOUT THIS BOOK...

WHY IS IT I never thought I would be a senior citizen? Now that I am one, I realize that others share this journey, which prompted the writing of this devotional book. God's truths are for everyone, no matter what our age, but those of us who are seniors can benefit from one another's wisdom as we journey together on this unfamiliar road.

This book is divided into fifty-two weeks. Each entry has a specific topic with questions for each day or a general question for the week. There is space to write your answers, comments, or notes. There is no set order to the presentation of each week, except those specified as holiday weeks.

Because it can be easy to forget a daily reading or devotional, I suggest that you read each week's devotion every morning. This will provide you with an opportunity to keep it in your mind and record how God spoke to you at the end of each day.

God's blessings!
Diane

CONTENTS

HEART LESSONS

GOD'S WORD

AGING

GRACEFULLY?

Read: Psalm 92:12-15

Wisdom is with aged men, With long life is understanding.
(Job 12:12)

THERE WAS A little card on my mother's dressing table that I remember seeing through the years. I believe it was a slogan provided by a make-up company. It read something like this: "I don't intend to grow old gracefully, I intend to fight it every step of the way!" In some ways, that's a good attitude to abide by, to keep mind and body as healthy and active as possible, but there also must be an acceptance that the aging process is how God created us, and his plan includes changes that we must receive gracefully and thankfully, especially how we age physically. In addition, we must face aging as it relates to our career, an empty nest, retirement, and a host of other changes that are all part of this journey.

As I reflect on King David's life, I find many good examples of how he handled issues of aging with grace. David's heart desire was to build a house for God, but God told him, "…your son who will be born to you, he will build the house in My name" (1 Kings 8:19). Years later, when he was almost killed in battle, David's men asked him to hang up his sword. It was difficult for David to admit that he was no longer the great and mighty warrior he had once been. His wisdom in leading the nation was to be wherever his nation needed him, not on the battlefield (2 Samuel 21:15-17). When David neared the end of his life, he made sure that his son, Solomon, was on the throne and prepared with all he needed to build the temple. In 1 Kings 2:1-9 David's last words to his son are recorded, his affairs now in order. As he lay dying, perhaps the hardest change to accept was when a young girl had to be found to keep him warm because covers alone were not adequate in his advanced years (1 Kings 1:1-4).

Many seniors have been healthy, independent and self-sufficient for so long that they fight against help of any kind, making life unpleasant and difficult for their loved ones, and perhaps even themselves. As we age, we must use the examples of David, the mighty warrior and king, to admit to ourselves the changes needed to embrace God's plan for our senior years.

Prayer:

Father God, as I am aging, help me to realize that I don't have the strength or health "to do it all." I don't need to dig in my heels and protest the help that I may require, or the changes you want me to make. Help me to grow old gracefully, be a blessing to my loved ones, and bring you the glory. Amen

Thought for the Week:

I want to be remembered as someone who grew old gracefully.

Questions to Reflect Upon:

Monday:
In what ways are you fighting the aging process? Is this fight harmful to your body or spirit in any way?

Tuesday:
What process of aging have you accepted?

Wednesday:
What process of aging are you not accepting?

Thursday:
Think of someone who is older that you admire. How has this person grown old gracefully?

Friday:
What is your attitude going to be if and when you are totally dependent on others?

Saturday:
Do you think David aged gracefully?

Sunday:
Think of another biblical character who aged gracefully.

AN INSIDE PASSAGE

Read: 2 Corinthians 4:17-18

"For I know the plans I have for you," declares the Lord, "plans for welfare
and not for calamity to give you a future and a hope."
(Jeremiah 29:11)

THINK OF A time when it seemed so important for you to know the future. As a
senior citizen, I want to know how long I will live, if I will have fairly good health,
and if I will possess a sound mind. We wonder about many things, but in reality, it would
not be good to know these answers. It has often been said that if we could see everything
that would happen in our lives, we would not be able to handle it. We would opt to end
it all before one more day dawned.

God does provide us with a glimpse of possibility that may or may not happen.
A teachable moment or a specific learning place can prepare us for whatever He has
planned. As we look to the future, it is important to remember that we will always have
his promises that cover all of the "what ifs."

Helping to care for my eighty-seven-year-old mom gave me a glimpse, or maybe
a wakeup call, to some of the physical changes I can most likely expect in the future.
My mom and I are the same size and build. As I helped her dress and shop for clothes,
I became aware of her aging, withering body, but the real shocker came when I took a
good look at my own aging, sagging body. I'm already on my way!

We get so caught-up in outward appearances that we live in denial that we will ever
be sagging and wrinkled. We spend time and money avoiding or trying to prevent what
is inevitable. More important than the outward passage of aging, is the inward passage. I
am a senior, but those who are even more senior give me a look into the inward passage
that I would do well to heed. I observe and know seniors who are so full of life and
ready for adventure, often in spite of physical limitations. I want to be that way, open
and ready for whatever is next in God's plan. I don't want to resist change or live in

fear of future "what ifs." Following the example of these active seniors will spur me on to finish strong.

Prayer:

Father God, as one of your seniors, help me to focus on what really counts. Rather than worry about the outward changes taking place, allow me to concentrate on the inward changes that you are working through me. Amen.

Thought for the Week:

Wrinkles and wisdom often go together.

Monday:
Ask yourself why you want to look years younger than you are.

Tuesday:
Will you be open to any major change God may have in store for you?

Wednesday:
What health "what ifs" are you concerned about?

Thursday:
Are you reaching out, looking for new adventures, and interests?

Friday:
What wisdom have you gained along with your addition of wrinkles?

Saturday:
Is there someone who could benefit from the wisdom of your life experiences?

Sunday:
Ask God to lead you to a younger person who needs mentoring.

OLD

Read: Psalm 71:17-18

Therefore we do not lose heart, but though our outer man is decaying,
yet our inner man is being renewed day by day.
(2 Corinthians 4:16)

AFTER THREE YEARS in the Navy, we came back home with a six-month-old daughter and moved into our first home. Across the street lived a sweet, elderly couple who welcomed us and were so helpful to a young couple with their first child. This past December, a young couple moved in across the street from us with *their* first child. With that occurrence came the shock that now *we* were the elderly couple across the street!

I had pushed the thought of ever being old from my conscious mind, yet slowly the reality of the aging process showed itself. The mirror didn't lie. Subtle health issues appeared, energy flagged, and then the faces of my parents stared back at me, "Old." I am afraid for them, but more so for myself, because I, too, am on my way "there." God's promise to me, however, is that he is renewing my inner man, in spite of what is happening to the outer one. God has always been more concerned with the issues of the heart and my relationship to him. In this aging process, he has promised to never leave me in the face of whatever lies ahead.

Prayer:

Father God, you cannot renew my "inner man" without my cooperation. May I be open to your will as you subtract the "old" in my life and add the "new" day-by-day. Amen.

Thought for the Week:

My neighbor says, "Still living, still learning!"
Are you still living? Are you still learning? What have you learned today?

Monday

Tuesday

Wednesday

Thursday

Friday

Saturday

Sunday

ROLE REVERSAL

Read: 1 Timothy 5:3-4

Honor your father and your mother that your days may be prolonged
in the land which the Lord your God gives you.
(Exodus 20:12)

I SPENT A week with my mother when I relieved my brother for a much-needed vacation. He was 24/7 caregiver for my mom, as an accident had left her unable to be left alone to care for herself. Needing to get out more to strengthen her weak legs, I was delighted when she agreed to come to church with me. As I helped her out of the car and walked her very slowly and carefully over rough areas in the pavement, I was struck by the fact that she had done the same for me when I was learning how to walk. Thinking of this brought to mind all the other ways she had served me as I now did my best to serve her. I cooked for her, helped her dress, and tried to keep her safe. We had reversed the roles, the child had become the mom to the mom.

At times, I would like to be a child again. I find comfort in being taken care of physically, but I know that the duties and responsibilities that are still part of my life are now God's plan for his continuing work in me. Yet, being taken care of in the sense of being loved and secure is, for me, being cared for. The promises of my heavenly Father are numerous as he cares for me, his child.

God has taken my mother home. I don't know what aging plan he has for me, but it may be to slip into that role my mom just left. Then I will be the aging parent looking to my children for whatever care I might need. With my heavenly Father, however, there will be no role reversal. I will always be his child.

Prayer:

Father God, as I cared for my mom, serving her as she served me, I was so grateful that I am your child. Your love is perfect and your care unending, and the irony of it all is that because of you, I grew up and matured to remain your child forever. Amen

Thought for the Week:

I will always be a child, his child.
In what ways are you God's child? Record one for each day.

Monday

Tuesday

Wednesday

Thursday

Friday

Saturday

Sunday

GRIEVING, BUT RELIEVED

Read: Psalm 30:10-12

But we do not want you to be uninformed, brethren, about those who are asleep, so that you will not grieve as do the rest, who have no hope.
(I Thessalonians 4:13)

IS IT POSSIBLE to feel relief and grief at the same time? Or does feeling both emotions lead to guilt, the equation being: GRIEF + RELIEF = GUILT?

When my mom passed away, or as I prefer to say, when she passed into life, I knew she was with Jesus. She had been failing for several years, physically and mentally, and my brother lived with her as her 24/7 caregiver. I helped him as much as I could, but he must feel some sort of relief even now, as he grieves, released from the burden he carried for so long.

I mourn for her too, missing the mom I remember before her health and mind began to fail. I also feel guilt, because I know I could have done more for both my brother and my mother.

It would be easier if we could separate emotions and experience them one at a time instead of such a mixture of grief, sorrow, relief, and yes, guilt—all wrapped up in love. As the days pass, I reflect on bits and pieces of life's memories with Mom. Sometimes it is a childhood incident, like the time I fell down the basement stairs and took a trip on the bus to see the doctor. Then there were those teenage years when I would beg to wear her sweaters. There were also times of mother-daughter conflict when rebellious words and actions come back to haunt me now. After my husband and I married and had children, she would frequently baby-sit the grandchildren so we could get away for a day or two. She was always generous to a fault, buying things for the children and us.

When the years of series of illnesses began, each one subtracted years from her life. The most difficult time of all was when she became confused, forgetful, and fearful. Until I learned to respond, I would argue with her, and now I live with feelings of guilt over those times. The painful mental picture to erase from my mind will be the last few hours of her life. That was not my mother in that hospital bed! I'm asking God to take that memory from my mind and replace it with one when she was full of life, always fun to be with.

Grieving involves so many emotions, and I believe the Lord allows us to experience them all, good and bad, as he brings each one to mind. We thank him for the good ones and the sad ones, and if necessary, ask forgiveness for the ones in which we caused pain and unhappiness to others.

I feel grief because my mom is gone, but relief that she is with the Lord, no longer confused, lonely, or in pain. As Paul said, "I …prefer rather to be absent from the body and to be at home with the Lord" (2 Corinthians 5:8).

Prayer:

Father, thank you for my mom. Bring all the good memories to mind. Forgive those times I was unkind to her. May this time of grieving bring more joy than sorrow, because I know she is with you. Amen

Thought for the Week:

Reflect on the good times

If you have lost one or both parents, or if they are still living, reflect on good memories. List one for each day.

Monday

Tuesday

Wednesday

Thursday

Friday

Saturday

Sunday

JEST PASSIN' THROUGH

Read: Acts 15:3

For while I was passing through and examining the objects of your worship,
I also found an altar with this inscription, 'TO AN UNKNOWN GOD.'
What therefore you worship in ignorance, this I proclaim to you.
(Acts 17:23)

IN THE WESTERN movies, I remember as a child, the gunslinger would ride into town alone. Hitching his horse outside the saloon, he would slowly enter the swinging doors and amble up to the bar. All action and conversation ceased as all eyes turned on the stranger.

The bartender would ask, "Haven't seen you in these parts before. Where ya headed, or are you plannin' to stay?"

The gunslinger would respond, "I'm jest passin' through."

Paul, in many of his missionary journeys, was doing just that, "passin' through." As he traveled through towns to spread the gospel, sometimes his presence started riots. But there were also times when he shared with other believers what had been occurring as he shared the gospel. "Therefore, being sent on their way by the church, they were passing through both Phoenicia and Samaria, describing in detail the conversion of the Gentiles, and were bringing great joy to all the brethren" (Acts 15:3). Paul was spreading the good news of conversions to other believers as he traveled through these areas. That must have been such an encouragement to believers. One of the more significant "passin' through" times was in Athens as Paul stood in the midst of the Areopagus seeing the altar to "AN UNKNOWN GOD." He came to proclaim to them the God of creation and everything in it.

Our lives are journeys, and like Paul, we are missionaries. Wherever we pass through, we should leave something of Christ behind ...seeds that we've planted, new believers that we introduced to Christ, or maturing disciples whom we helped to grow in faith. Places, people, and circumstances should claim, "...the darkness is passing away, and the true Light is already shinning" (1 John. 2:8), because we have been there to spread the light and love of Christ that dwells in us.

How often are we unaware of the times when our actions or attitudes are far from what Christ would want us to leave behind? Irritation with sales clerks, impatience with long lines in stores, and lack of courtesy everywhere are often the trail we leave. Unlike the gunslinger, who just stops for a drink and continues on, leaving no impact, we can stop, even briefly, to share a kind word or helpful act to implant Christ's love.

Prayer:

Father, don't let me miss those opportunities to share your Word and your love when I'm "jest passin' through." I pray that the impact of you be left behind after I leave. Amen.

Thought for the Week:

As I pass through, may I leave a reminder or evidence of you.
How many places have I passed through this week and left a touch of Jesus?

Monday

Tuesday

Wednesday

Thursday

Friday

Saturday

Sunday

GOD'S GIFTS

ALWAYS AMAZED

Read: Job 9:1-10

He counts the number of the stars; He gives names to all of them.
(Psalm 147:4)

SUMMER OF 2006 brought ninety- to one hundred-degree temperatures daily in July. We camped at 8,500 feet mainly to get out of the scorching heat in the valley. We hiked one of the loops around our tallest peak of 10,776 feet. Two very wet winters left carpets of lush green meadows, blanketed with wild flowers of every variety and hue. Patches of snow still lingered and waterfalls and streams rushed everywhere. As we were coming around a bend to find a place to have lunch, we were greeted with a surprise—a spectacular waterfall! We had lunch with a view. I wouldn't trade that lunch spot in God's creation for all the trendy restaurants in the world.

I never tire of God's magnificent creation. Every detail is fascinating. My husband and I enjoy the ocean and combing the beach, but we are mountain people. Born and raised surrounded by mountains, I can't imagine living anywhere else. The plains just won't cut it for us.

Being out in God's creation, wherever and in whatever the season, brings to mind countless Scriptures. One that recently jumped out at me for the first time is when Job exclaims, "He stretches out the north over empty space. And hangs the earth on nothing" (Job 26:7). He hangs the earth on *nothing*! This was thousands of years before we thought we were so smart with our evolution and big bang theories. From our galaxy, which is one of many, to a single blade of grass, all we can see with the naked eye boggles the mind. Vegetation displays of flowers, trees, fruits, and vegetables—each have their own intricate designs and purpose. Pick up a leaf or examine a flower. Look closely at its complex structure. Psalm 104 speaks of different animals, even the sea monster, Leviathan. A trip to an aquarium provides just a small sampling of the many varieties of sea life and displays God's sense of humor! To this day, scientists continue to discover new species in remote places of the earth and in the depths of the oceans.

In Job 38-41, God quizzes Job by asking him many questions about creation, "Where were you when I laid the foundation of the earth" (Job 38:4a)! God also inquires of Job,

"Have you entered the storehouses of the snow, Or have you seen the storehouses of hail, Which I have reserved for the time of distress, For the day of war and battle" (Job 38:22-23)? Of his creation of the horse, God asks Job, "Do you give the horse his might? Do you clothe his neck with a mane" (Job 38:19)? God also asks, "Is it by your understanding that the hawk soars, stretching his wings toward the south" (Job 39:26).

The more we read passages in the Word and obverse God's handiwork, the more we know what our God is like and what an incredible "life with a view" we have.

Prayer:

Father, I am in awe and always amazed by your creation. May that serve to teach me more about you and worship you more as my Creator. Amen.

Thought for the Week:

Where was I when God laid the foundations of the earth?
Read Job 38-39

Reflections for each day:

Monday:
Find a Scripture in Job 38-39 that describes the weather today.

Tuesday:
Recall a time when you had "lunch with a view." How were you refreshed?

Wednesday:
What animal have you seen that made you wonder why God created it?

Thursday:
Go outside and really look for something in God's creation that you have never seen before. What was it?

Friday:
Read the thought for the week and then read Psalm 139 aloud.

Saturday:
As you read through Job 38-39, find at least one statement by God you never saw before.

Sunday:
Do the same as you did for Saturday

PALM PILOT

Read: Psalm 139:7-10

Behold, I have inscribed you on the palms of my hands;
Your walls are continually before me.
(Isaiah 49:16)

DO YOU FEEL as lost as I do in this fast moving, technological world? I still have not begun to master all that my computer can do, and it is a very slow moving dinosaur in today's computer world. Our daughter has been a part of this high-tech, corporate world for quite some time, and she has moved right along with all the upgrades and newest technology, taking everything to the next level, (whatever that means for her job).

The cell phone is still a wonder to me. I have one, but seldom use it. It is more for emergency purposes rather than text messaging, picture taking, contacts, and Internet access.

When I do have it on and it rings, I'm startled into a panic mode. Which button do I push to talk? What if I accidentally dial 911 or press any number of other things that could cause me undue embarrassment?

There is also the Palm Pilot. This small device fits in the palm of your hand and works as your daily planner. It is an address book, calendar, and can even find restaurants when you are out of town!

Our daughter's latest toy is a Treo 650! It is a cell phone and Palm Pilot rolled into one. It looks like a cell phone and has its own keyboard called "qwerty." (As of this writing, I realize this gadget is probably no longer the latest, but whatever it is, she will have it!)

Everything you need or want to do is right there in the palm of your hand. But batteries burn out, power can be lost, computer chips fail, all resulting in missing messages, phone connections cut off, and documents lost. We are also finding that all this technology has led to a lack of privacy, scams of all kinds, and worst of all, identity theft. Still, the Creator of everything, yes, even all these gadgets, never loses power, crashes, breaks, or misplaces a thing! In Isaiah, God tells us that we are inscribed in the palms of his hands. Wow! My identity in this world may be stolen, but the God who created me will never allow my identity to be stolen in his world. I am inscribed on the palm of his hand, and for that matter, written in the Lamb's book of life forever (Revelation 21:27)! Hallelujah!

Prayer:

Father God, in this fast moving world of so much mind-boggling technology that can leave me feeling insecure and even fearful, I thank you for keeping me in the palm of your hand, never to be removed. May you remind me of this every time I see a Palm Pilot. Amen.

Thought for the Week:

"My soul clings to You; Your right hand upholds me" (Psalm 63:8).

Consult a concordance. Read a Scripture about God's hand and record what it means to you every day this week.

Monday

Tuesday

Wednesday

Thursday

Friday

Saturday

Sunday

RARE MOMENTS

Read: Mark 9:2-4

Peter said to Jesus, "Rabbi, it is good for us to be here; let us
make three tabernacles, one for You, and one for Moses, and one for Elijah.
(Mark 9:5)

THE INDIANAPOLIS 500 is the pinnacle achievement of open wheel racing. Winning this race is what every race driver dreams of accomplishing. Indy cars, or the IRL series, have a yearly championship winner determined by points earned during the racing season. Points are awarded for being on the pole, leading laps, finishing in the top ten, and of course, winning the race. A few drivers have won the championship and even the Indy 500 several times. Others have only won a race or two in their entire career, and some have never even won at all. The championship and the Indy 500 are mountaintop experiences, each one unique, which cannot ever be repeated. But each driver will tell you they continue to pursue the win in each race. I've often wondered how the emotional experience differs when a driver wins the Indy 500 for the second time. Is it the same exhilarating, euphoric feeling?

In our spiritual journey, we too, have those mountaintop experiences. Even though we hope for a repeat of feelings and emotions, we know it won't happen again. It can be crippling to our walk, waiting for the spectacular to happen in the same way it did the first time. If we always long for those mountaintop experiences, we will accomplish nothing in the valley. As Oswald Chambers said, "The proof that we are rightly related to God is that we do our best whether we feel inspired or not." We build our characters out of everyday duties and obedience to whatever God has called us to at the moment. The emotional high of being on the mountaintop is for God's specific purpose and will differ with each circumstance. Expectations of an identical or similar experience will only bring disappointment, and we will have missed what God intended for us in the valley. Rare moments are God's surprises.

Prayer:

Father, may what you teach me on the mountain be brought down to the valley. May I not long for the same experience, but wait and watch for something new. Amen

Thought for the Week:

Surprise me, God.
How has God surprised you this week?

Monday

Tuesday

Wednesday

Thursday

Friday

Saturday

Sunday

PUZZLES

Read: Colossians 1:25-27

…that their hearts may be encouraged, having been knit together in love, and attaining to all the wealth that comes from the full assurance of understanding, resulting in a true knowledge of God's mystery, that is, Christ Himself, in whom are hidden all the treasures of wisdom and knowledge.
(Colossians 2:2-3)

EVERY YEAR, USUALLY between Christmas and New Years, my husband and I enjoy doing a jigsaw puzzle. We often do a one thousand piece puzzle of a beautiful scene or perhaps a more unrealistic picture with very involved detail and color. The one we did this year was of Mt. Rushmore in South Dakota. Besides the face of the several Presidents carved in the rocks, there were also a train, several air balloons in the sky, pine trees, and many groups of people doing a variety of activities. It was a very interesting but challenging puzzle! At times, it seemed overwhelming, but as the pieces began to fit together, specific areas of the picture appeared. It was amazing to me as I struggled with piecing together swirls of pink, white, cream and tan that suddenly a face of a president appeared. When the last piece was put in place, we saw many details we hadn't seen before in addition to the completed picture.

I thought about this as God reveals parts to the puzzle of what he is doing in our lives. The mystery of ages past is revealed to us in Christ, which brought us to him to be saved. There are also life's trials and tests that are also a part of the puzzle. At those times, God has chosen to reveal another piece of the puzzling mystery in life. Looking back on those trials and tests, we can see how that puzzle piece completed a part of our puzzle, revealing more of how God works in our lives and shows us who he is in Christ Jesus.

We receive another piece of the mysterious puzzle to our future when we physically die. "Behold, I tell you a mystery; we shall not all sleep, but we shall all be changed, in a moment, in the twinkling of an eye, at the last trumpet; for the trumpet will sound, and the dead will be raised imperishable, and we shall be changed" (1 Corinthians 15:51-52). "For the Lord Himself will descend from heaven with a shout, with the voice of the archangel and with the trumpet of God, and the dead in Christ shall rise first. Then we who are alive and remain shall be caught up together with them in the clouds to meet the Lord in the air, and so we shall always be with the Lord" (1 Thessalonians 4:16-17). We are thankful for this mystery, this part of the puzzle being revealed to us, but we don't have the completed picture between now and then. When we are in heaven, we will see and understand how the pieces fit together.

Prayer:

Father God, often the puzzle pieces of my life don't seem to fit anywhere! Help me to trust you that every detail of my life has been planned out, and it will all fit together perfectly at the end of my life. Amen.

Thought for the Week:

The final mystery has been solved! Recall a time when what God was doing made no sense. But now, as you look back, you see how that piece of the puzzle fits.

Monday

Tuesday

Wednesday

Thursday

Friday

Saturday

Sunday

ROCKS

Read 2 Samuel 22:2-7

I love You, O Lord, my strength. The Lord is my rock and my fortress and my
deliverer, My God, my rock, in whom I take refuge; My shield and
the horn of my salvation, my stronghold.
(Psalm 18:1-2)

THE TAHOE RIM Trail is still a work in progress as many work to create a hiking trail around God's awesome creation called Lake Tahoe. On a beautiful Fourth of July, we hiked a portion of this trail taking in the glory of it all. In one area, we came upon rocks that resembled giant ice cubes God had tumbled out of ice trays. We left the trail to move closer and explore these rocks. There were many crevices that allowed someone to find shelter. In one place, there were two huge rocks covered by a flat one. God had even provided a roof!

As we investigated this area of God's protection and covering for man and animals alike, I was reminded of all the places in his Word that told of God being our Rock. In the Psalms, David calls God his Rock, Shelter, and Fortress at least twenty-four times. In Exodus and Numbers, water came out of the rock, and Paul refers to this in 1 Corinthians 10:4, stating that the rock was Christ. In many places in the Old Testament, rocks are used as altars and reminders of what God had done for his people. In Exodus, God hides Moses in the cleft of the rock. In the New Testament, Jesus uses a picture of building on the rock as a strong foundation, utilizing him as that rock and chief cornerstone.

When I am afraid, worried, or stressed, I need to think of those huge rock formations and the protection and safety they provide. They will be reminders that he who created them is far greater.

Prayer:

Father God, Creator of all, remind me of your protection and show me that you are in control. Just like David, I can call you my Rock, trusting that you will be my Fortress for whatever I'm going through. Amen.

Thought for the Week:

I need to look at more rocks!
For each day, find a Scripture where God is described as a rock.

Monday

Tuesday

Wednesday

Thursday

Friday

Saturday

Sunday

ABIDING

LOCATION, LOCATION, LOCATION

Read: Psalm 91:1

"Just as the Father has loved Me, I have also loved you; abide in My love."
(John 15:9)

THE BOLD PRINT of the ad shouts, "Location, location, location!" if you are looking to buy real estate. The price, whether a house, business or lot, depends on this detail. The price of a modest size house can become astronomical if it's on a golf course, in a quiet wooded area, or with a scenic view of a lake, river, or ocean. A desirable area always has a premium price tag. While house hunting, we looked at a house that fell into that category. It was a darling 30s-40s era house in a well-kept older part of town. It needed a kitchen renovation, a new furnace, and the sixty-year-old plumbing and wiring had to be dealt with. The rest of the house was in good condition and in an ideal part of town, but it certainly reflected an exorbitant price tag for what the house needed in order to be livable.

As we mature as Christians, we can look at where we are in our relationship with Jesus in the same way as we look at where we live. Is our place with him prime property or are we on the fringe—just on the outer edges of somewhere? Do we need to move closer in? Location, location, location becomes the all-important key to relationship, relationship, relationship. When Jesus says, "Abide in me," isn't this the most prestigious abode of all, to live with the King of Kings and Lord of Lords? We might not always live in the same physical dwelling, but we will always abide in him. There is no price tag on this house, because he paid it all so that we can always live in the best neighborhood.

Prayer:

Father God, thank you for always providing the best place in which I may dwell with you. Amen.

Thought for the week:

Location equates to relationship with God.
At the end of each day, ask yourself, "When did I not abide in him?"

Monday

Tuesday

Wednesday

Thursday

Friday

Saturday

Sunday

THE PIANO CRATE

Read: Psalm 84:1-4

I was glad when they said to me, "Let us go into the house of the Lord."
(Psalm 122:1)

WHEN I WAS a child, my dad and uncle owned a music store. It was a special place for us to visit. Usually on a Saturday morning, my brother and I would take the bus downtown for the morning movies with an admittance price of a milk bottle cap! After the movies, right around the corner, was the music store where my aunt helped out. We could sometimes talk her into taking us to lunch and let us take a Bozo the Clown record home. The best part of all was when the store received a shipment of pianos and organs. They would come in large, wooden crates, and we would claim two of them for the back yard. What fun we had and how our imaginations ran wild, as the crates became a jungle house, a log cabin, or a secret hide-a-way. Sometimes we even played church.

The other morning on my walk, I saw a large, wooden crate. All of those childhood memories of the fun we had in the backyard came flooding back. We felt so safe and secure in our crate. I feel that way when I am in the Lord's places of worship. He created so many places for us in which to worship and dwell in his presence: magnificent cathedrals, storefronts, living rooms, the many places in which missionaries abroad find themselves, and one of my favorites— anywhere outside in his glorious creation.

Johannes Brahms may have been thinking of the many dwelling places of God when he composed the *German Requiem*. It is unlike any other requiem. Other composers followed the mass for the dead as a pattern for their requiem. Brahms however, composed his requiem for the living, as a comfort for those who had lost a loved one. The fourth movement of the requiem is taken from Psalm 84 and is titled, "How Lovely is Thy Dwelling Place." How lovely it is to dwell in the house of the Lord as we look to our future dwelling place in heaven!

Prayer:

Father God, I'm overwhelmed with your love for me and all the places I may dwell with you, anywhere, anytime. May I dwell each day with you. Amen

Thought for the Week:

"Lord, You have been our dwelling place in all generations. Before the mountains were born or You gave birth to the earth and the world, Even from everlasting to everlasting, You are God" (Psalm 90:1-2).

Are you able to dwell everywhere with the Lord? Each evening recall those places where you dwelt with him during the day.

Monday

Tuesday

Wednesday

Thursday

Friday

Saturday

Sunday

WRITTEN IN PENCIL

Read Ephesians 2:19-22

So then you are no longer strangers and aliens, but you are fellow citizens
with the saints, and are of God's household, …
(Ephesians 2:19)

AS I WAS addressing Christmas cards, I was amazed at all of the changes in addresses this last year. Entries in the address book written in pen were crossed out and relocated to the bottom of the page or on the next one. Some that were written in pencil had been erased and changed several times, and sadly, those whose names would not be on an envelope this year had passed away. Out of our five children, four changed addresses this year, one changed within the same state, two moved to different states, and one just moved across town, newly married. The New Year will see three of these children change addresses yet again. Our eldest daughter and husband will make their new address a forty-five-foot yacht in San Francisco Bay. That is really a change of address! Whew! Mom and Dad, however, have had the same address for thirty years. It is a sign of our times and our children's generation. After this year, I think a new address book is in order with all addresses and names written in pencil.

All of this transiency reminds me of the temporary home we have here on earth. We are aliens here, and this is not our home (1 Peter 1:1). Heaven, in the presence of Jesus, is our final and permanent residence. We won't need to pack, move or create address changes! There will be no adjustments to anything, as we will fit right in, comfortable and at home in a place created just for us. If it were not so, Jesus says he would have told us (John 14:2). Our lives here on earth are written in pencil, but in heaven, they are written in permanent ink in the Book of Life (Luke 10:20, Philippians 4:3). Hallelujah!

Prayer:

Father God, in a world that is temporary and passing away, our addresses change. But your address for us in heaven is forever. May I remember that when I'm feeling insecure over any type of change. Amen.

Thought for the Week:

Make sure your address is written in indelible ink!

Ask God to remind you where your permanent address is located each day this week.

Monday

Tuesday

Wednesday

Thursday

Friday

Saturday

Sunday

CHANGES

IT'S JUST A HOUSE

Read: Psalm 90:1-2

The curse of the Lord is on the house of the wicked,
But He blesses the dwelling of the righteous.
(Proverbs 3:33)

IT'S JUST A house. This may be true for some, those who have moved every few years and don't have the tendency to get emotionally attached. However, it is a real shocker when you decide to move after thirty years in the same home!

We've been talking about downsizing, not only our stuff, but the size of our house as well. All five children are married and have relocated, several of them across the country. So that left just the two of us with a huge house and a huge yard.

When we finally made the decision to move, it was traumatic, not only for us, but for our children as well. I knew the move would affect all of them in some way as they saw their family home where they created their childhood memories go to a new owner. I was surprised when I found out that they had been frantically burning up long distance minutes crisscrossing the country with their calls to each other to see if they could get together and buy the house themselves.

We kept running into friends who were also thinking about making the move to downsize. One friend told us that her daughter, who lives in town, was very distressed and commented, "I will be so upset to drive down the street and know that someone else is living in our house."

My friend replied, "Well, don't drive down the street." (What a great one-liner!)

The Lord gave us this house, and it had been a blessing, not only to our family, but also to over fifty foster children. There were many church gatherings that took place at the house, from Bible studies to potlucks. The inanimate wood and bricks contain all of those wonderful memories of family life, both the joys and the sorrows. Thinking of all the years in that house reminded me once again that it all took place because of God. Our house was always a peaceful place of refuge, in spite of whatever circumstance we were going through. We had experienced all of those good times because of God's presence, his Spirit dwelling in our home.

As we made a new beginning in a much smaller house, we once again found his Spirit there. His Spirit will always fill our home. It really doesn't matter how large or small, tent or mansion, wherever God is, a home can be.

Prayer:

Father God, please help me to remember that it doesn't matter where I live, as long as I always dwell in you. Amen,

Thought for the Week:

Home is where God is!

Reflect on each house you have lived in. Which ones were filled with his Spirit? Which ones were not?

Monday

Tuesday

Wednesday

Thursday

Friday

Saturday

Sunday

LET GO, PUT ASIDE

Read Galatians 1:15-17

For this reason also, since the day we heard of it, we have not ceased to pray
for you and to ask that you may be filled with the knowledge of His will in all
spiritual wisdom and understanding, …
(Colossians 1:9)

THE DAY HAD arrived; choir would begin without me as director. My heart hurt. It
was the same emotion that I had experienced on the first day of a new semester when
I was not in the classroom because God had made it clear that my teaching days needed
to end. Why is change so hard? In the last few years, God has asked me to let go of work
and certain areas of service. I have always been a music person: teaching, directing, and
performing. After letting go of teaching and directing the choir, God gave me a new call
to serve as the part-time director at the Crisis Pregnancy Center, but soon that changed
too. I was now no longer on staff at the center, but back on as a volunteer counselor. This
was God's timing to be more involved in the care of our "antique" moms.

After the Apostle Paul's conversion, he was set aside in Arabia, (Galatians 1:17), for
a time to listen to God, to be taught all that was needed for what God had planned for
him. I felt that way then, set aside to listen and allow God to teach me. I have learned
a great deal in caring for our moms, especially in the area of emotional need. It has
been a completely new lesson for me in service, and I must also add, a place I never
envisioned myself.

When we say, "I'll do whatever you want, Lord," we don't get to pick where or how
we will serve. It may not be a fun, comfortable place, where the ego can be fed! We must
listen carefully, waiting for the next step, recognizing what God has done and what he is
doing now. Every moment of our day is a part of his plan, even when it seems as though
nothing is happening at all.

Prayer:

Father, I know that there is nothing in our lives that happens to us that is wasted. You have used me through it all. I have let go of those areas where I have served in obedience. I ask for strength, insight, and much joy as you bring me into another new place to serve you. Amen.

Thought for the Week:

If I serve out of who I think I am, I am not serving you.

As you go through the week, be aware of changes, big and small, that God may be asking you to make.

Monday

Tuesday

Wednesday

Thursday

Friday

Saturday

Sunday

LOOK AHEAD, NOT BEHIND

Read Isaiah 43:18-19

Brethren, I do not regard myself as having laid hold of it yet; but one thing I do: forgetting what lies behind and reaching forward to what lies ahead, I press on toward the goal for the prize of the upward call of God in Christ Jesus.
(Philippians 3:13-14)

NOSTALGIA—HOW IT creeps up on me! I thought the decision of changing careers was behind me. *No problem*, I thought as I laid it down knowing God was in it and calling me to something different. But a year later, I was back in the physical environment that I had "laid down." After fourteen years in the university setting, first as a student and then as instructor, I was now back on campus for a series of award receptions and a concert. The emotions of desire to be back on campus were overwhelming. It even crossed my mind to call the head of the music department and ask if I could teach a class again. But God intervened, speaking to my heart of the change he had orchestrated. He reminded me to forget those things that lie behind, not in the sense never to remember or forget what he taught me through those experiences, but to "press on" to the new things he had in store for me.

I need to lay aside the emotions and feelings of that part of my life a second time. They may come again, tempting me to become nostalgic and long for the past, but I know that God will remind me to look ahead to what he has planned for the future.

Prayer:

Father, help me to remember but not long for the past. Focus me forward so I don't miss what you have planned for me now. "...now it will spring forth..." Amen

Thought for the Week:

Looking back, while moving forward, can cause us to fall!
Does nostalgia trip you up? In what areas do you long for the past?

Monday

Tuesday

Wednesday

Thursday

Friday

Saturday

Sunday

MIRROR, MIRROR ON THE WALL

Read: Proverbs 31:10-31, 1 Peter 3:3-4

…for God sees not as a man sees, for man looks at the outward appearance,
but the Lord looks at the heart.
(1 Samuel 16:7b)

IT IS STRESSFUL to be intimidated with beautiful faces and bodies that we are expected to pattern ourselves after, especially for those who do not possess the beauty or good looks that turn heads. This worldly pressure can be very strong and quite subtle. Magazines, movies, and television are constantly showing us what we are supposed to look like. For women, it is a model-thin figure with long, luxurious locks and no wrinkles! A man must have a buff body that reflects hours at the gym and some sort of hair rejuvenation if he is going bald. Scripture cautions that God looks at the heart, not at our outward appearance. It is disconcerting to find many places in the Bible that record a person's outward appearance. The Bible calls Sari, Abram's wife, a very beautiful woman. Rebekah is mentioned as being a very beautiful girl and Rachel as beautiful in form and face. The Bible calls Abigail intelligent as well as beautiful in appearance. Bathsheba is mentioned as being intelligent as well as beautiful, and Esther is revealed as beautiful in form and face. Male Bible characters that are recorded as handsome are: Moses as a baby, David as a boy, Joseph, Saul and David's son, Absolom.

Isaiah 53:2 says this about Jesus, "For He grew up before Him like a tender shoot, and like a root out of parched ground; He has no stately form or majesty That we should look upon Him, Nor appearance that we should be attracted to Him." It wasn't his appearance that attracted people to Jesus, it was his compassion and the authority emanating through him (Matthew 7:29).

If it wasn't important for Jesus to be physically beautiful, why is it important to us? Especially as we grow older and begin to lose whatever beauty or attractiveness we have, it is important to focus on the inner beauty of Christ's life in us. The inner beauty shines forth in the fruit of the spirit. Not that we are to neglect the temple of the Holy Spirit, but we must always focus and base our self-worth in Christ and nothing else.

Prayer:

Father, forgive me for always being over concerned and comparing my outward appearance to others. May I focus on the inward beauty of my life in you. Amen,

Thought for the Week:

Mirror, mirror on the wall, Christ is the beauty in us all!

When others see you, do they see the Christ in you? For each day of the week, reflect on a Christ-like characteristic that you want God to work in you. Ask him to show you how to accomplish this.

Monday

Tuesday

Wednesday

Thursday

Friday

Saturday

Sunday

FOUR LESSONS FROM
A HORIZONTAL POSITION

Read: 2 Corinthians 1:3-5, 7

…and our hope for you is firmly grounded, knowing that as you are sharers of
our sufferings, so also you are sharers of our comfort.
(2 Corinthians 1:7)

RECONSTRUCTIVE SURGERY ON my foot put a very different perspective on everything, especially those daily activities. My out-of-commission foot played such a subconscious significance that I was now rendered almost totally helpless. Learning to use crutches, bathing, and just getting up and down out of bed or a chair presented a great deal of conscious physical thought and effort. The kitchen became a particularly arduous place to function on crutches. One early revelation was being unable to carry anything while on crutches. Like a toddler learning to go up and down stairs, I was on my bottom, dragging my crutches behind.

Apart from all the inconvenience and amusing aspects of this process, the Lord was teaching me some new, valuable lessons. One of the hardest lessons for me, being a "Martha" personality, was to cease all physical activity. This has always been a struggle for me, to let go, sit at his feet, and listen. Yet I know that no household things I do are important in comparison to opportunities I have to deepen my relationship with God.

The second lesson I learned was the physical aspect of healing. Even though this was just a small window into physical healing time, it does give greater insight into the suffering of those who have had tragic accidents and injuries with months and even years of recuperation. It does bring me up short with my few short months of healing.

A third lesson that was brought into sharper focus came from 2 Corinthians 1:3-5. It says that as Christ comforts us in our affliction, we, in turn, will be able to comfort others who are in affliction. As I recently noticed in verse four, we have been comforted, "…so that we may be able to comfort those who are in ANY affliction…." The experience doesn't have to be the same, but it is Christ's comfort that is the same, no matter what the circumstances.

The fourth and most significant lesson was enduring the physical pain. I wonder how much I will be able to bear when put to another possible test in any type of physical affliction. Going a step beyond that, will I be able, if called upon, to suffer torture and pain in my stand for Christ?

Prayer:

Father God, thank you for those lessons learned in the time of pain. May they give me more compassion to comfort others in their suffering. Amen

Thought for the Week:

Pain brings us closer to God.

Recall times when you have been physically or emotionally down. Record a specific time each day. What did you learn? How was it useful to comfort others?

Monday

Tuesday

Wednesday

Thursday

Friday

Saturday

Sunday

VESSELS

Read: Isaiah 29:16

On the contrary, who are you, O man, who answers back to God? The thing
molded will not say to the molder, "Why did you make me like this, will it?"
Or does not the potter have a right over the clay, to make from the same
lump one vessel for honorable use, and another for common use?
(Romans 9:20-21)

MY SISTER-IN-LAW IS a master potter and teacher. She has made a special bowl, mug, and other pieces for each family unit. They are beautifully shaped, molded, glazed and fired in rich colors. What makes these so unique are the slight imperfections that speak of being handcrafted in love, not stamped out in an assembly line. When we received one of these lovely pieces for Christmas, God brought to mind the many places in Scripture where he is referred to as the potter and we the clay. Up coming changes in my life prompted a conversation with the Lord.

"O, yes, Lord, You can mold me anyway you want, whatever type of vessel to be used as you desire. I am clay in your hands."

"O, really?" asks the Lord. "Are you ready to come out of the spotlight and have the shape of teacher and choir director completely refashioned into a vessel to serve your elderly mother and mother-in-law?"

How often I have nodded my head in agreement with the familiar Jeremiah passage that provides a picture of the Potter and the clay (Jeremiah 18:4-6). But in reality, I'm still struggling with the Potter when he wants to mold me into a new vessel that I don't think I can be and may not even wish to be! "Woe to the one who quarrels with his Maker—An earthenware vessel among the vessels of the earth! Will the clay say to the potter, 'What are you doing?' Or the thing you are making say, 'He has no hands'" (Isaiah 45:9)?

Through time, others have struggled with the same issue, telling the Potter what to do, what to make, and how to go about it. But is not God the sovereign creator of all? Our Father really does know best and since he holds the copyright, he can alter a vessel at anytime in appearance or use it as he sees fit for his use, not ours. It really doesn't matter what the vessel is, because it says in 2 Corinthians 4:7, "But we have this treasure in earthen vessels, so that the surpassing greatness of the power will be of God and not of ourselves."

Prayer:

Father God, you do hold the copyright and original blueprint to my very formation. I acknowledge that you have the right to change anything at anytime with the original plan. Bring this knowledge from my head to my heart. Amen.

Thought for the Week:

> Have Thine own way, Lord Have Thine own way,
> Thou art the Potter: I am the clay.
> Mold me and make me After Thy will,
> While I am waiting Yielded and still.
>
> —Adelaide A. Pollard

Read Isaiah 64:8. How has God shown you where you are trying to mold yourself into something he never intended you to be this week?

Monday

Tuesday

Wednesday

Thursday

Friday

Saturday

Sunday

RELATIONSHIPS

THE WHISPERER

Read: 1 Kings 19:9-14

Be still and know that I am God;...
(Psalm 46:10a NIV)

THE MOVIE, *THE Horse Whisperer*, is a fascinating movie based on a true story. The horse whisperer controlled and tamed wild horses or horses with an attitude problem, by his quiet, gentle ways. Recently, the same technique has been applied to dogs. *The Dog Whisperer* is a television show promoting a person who uses similar tactics in dealing with out of control dogs. Thinking back on child rearing, I remember when I used a quiet, soft response or instruction. It always made much more of an impact than yelling.

As we read God's Word, we find he deals with us in much the same way. In 1 Kings 19, Elijah is running away from the evil Jezebel. He stops and is in a cave when the Lord speaks to him. Elijah tells God that he is finished being a prophet, and he wants to die. God tells him to go stand on the mountain before the Lord. The Lord passed by. There was a strong wind, earthquake, and fire, but the Lord was not in them. Yet when Elijah heard the sound of a gentle blowing, he heard God.

When Jesus needed to hear from his Father during his earthly ministry, he drew away from the crowds and his disciples to pray and listen to the Father. After Paul's encounter with Christ on the road to Damascus, Jesus sent him to Arabia for instruction. The Arabian Desert was certainly a place of silence and provided a time to listen and be taught (Galatians 1:17).

Extended times of complete silence are almost nonexistent in our culture. We really have to fight for those times to be with our heavenly Father. If the radio, CD player, ipod, and television are blaring in our ears, how will we ever hear God speak to us?

Psalm 46:10a says, "Be still and know I am God;..." knowing that he will reveal his will to us. Most of the time, it is hard enough to keep our thoughts focused on God and much harder with all the outside noise and distraction, but when we make the effort to find a quiet place, we will be amazed at what we hear in the silence.

Prayer:

Father, I desire with my whole heart to hear you speak to me. Help me to clear out all the distractions that keep me from listening. Allow me to be like Samuel and say, "Speak, for your servant is listening" (1 Samuel 3:10). Amen.

Thought for the Week:

Only in silence will you hear the *whisperer*.
Make time each day this week to listen in silence. What did you hear God say?

Monday

Tuesday

Wednesday

Thursday

Friday

Saturday

Sunday

CALVARY LOVE

Read Philippians 2:3-5, 4:8-9

So, as those who have been chosen of God, holy and beloved, put on a heart
of compassion, kindness, humility, gentleness and patience; bearing with one
another, and forgiving each other, whoever has a complaint against anyone;
just as the Lord forgave you, so also should you.
(Colossians 3:12-13)

IT WAS OVER. The 2004 elections for president and many other offices, both federal
and local, were finally over. The aftermath of the storm continued on. It was bitter on
the surface with character assassination, incidents of a personal nature from the past that
had nothing to do with current issues, and accusations of promises not kept. Beneath the
surface, a spiritual battle was waged. God's plan always wins regardless of who we think
should have been elected. We can get caught up in jokes and snide comments about the
candidates that circle through e-mails, work places, and social gatherings both before and
after an election. Anger and bitterness over election results can divide friends, neighbors,
families, and our country.

I wonder how many times my impression of someone has been colored in a negative
way because of something that was said about that person by another? It may even
cause me to avoid that person. But if I make the decision to find out the truth about
someone that was talked about, I will often be surprised as my entire impression changes
to positive.

Not only in circumstances such as these, but always as a Christian, I must guard
my thoughts, words, and actions in light of whose child I am. There is a quote by Amy
Carmichael, a missionary to India, that cuts to the heart motive, "If I can enjoy a joke
at the expense of another; if I can in any way slight another in conversation, or even in
thought, then I know nothing of Calvary love." That says it all.

Prayer:

Father God, how little I comprehend the magnitude of Calvary love. Continue to put a guard over my mouth and even more than that, may I bring all of my thoughts into captivity and obedience to Christ (2 Corinthians 10:5). May the cross be forever before me. Amen.

Thoughts for the Week:

CONVICTS

They rattle around,
prisoners in chains,
the thoughts in my mind.

But I fear they will break out,
a rioting rampage
of works and actions.

Escaped wicked thoughts,
that should have been executed…
long ago …by me.

Each day this week, record a misguided thought about another person. Confess it and ask God to replace it with his guidance.

Monday

Tuesday

Wednesday

Thursday

Friday

Saturday

Sunday

SUFFERING

Read: Philippians 2:1-2

So, as those who have been chosen of God, holy and beloved, put on a heart of
compassion, kindness, humility, gentleness and patience …
(Colossians 3:12)

THERE ARE MANY to whom God has given the gifts of mercy and compassion. They
jump into a crisis situation instinctively knowing what to do and say, ministering
to the deepest needs of those in pain. They don't shrink back from the sights and smells
of physical suffering or from the behavioral manifestations of emotional outbursts. I
am not one of those people. I don't like to make hospital visits, go to rest homes, or
mental institutions. I shrink back from the unpleasant, the abnormal, and anyone who is
suffering. I will always pray for them, but at a distance. Being this way causes me much
grief and feelings of guilt. Why am I like this? Dialogue from a novel I read many years
ago brings me some insight. In the novel, Mary's aunt has just passed away, and Mary
and the caregiver are speaking of the aunt's suffering which was mental in nature.

"Most of us tend to belittle all suffering except our own," said Mary. "I think it's fear.
We don't want to come too near in case we're sucked in and have to share it" (*The Scent
of Water* by Elizabeth Goudge).

I ought to share in the sufferings of others. Jesus, who is always our example to
follow, never shirked from reaching out and touching the sick in body and mind. He had
compassion for everyone. His response was that he came to do the Father's will. I am
to be obedient to whatever Jesus calls me to do. The excuse that I don't have those gifts
of mercy and compassion won't wash with him. Our lack of compassion and avoidance
to the suffering of others boils down to a lack of trust that God is all we need in any
situation. If he calls me to do what I think I can't do, I must obey and trust him to do in
me whatever is lacking …namely have a compassionate heart.

Prayer:

Father, when you call me to go, may I go with your heart of compassion. Amen.

Thought for the Week:

Just go. God will provide what you need.
If God calls you this week to visit someone who is ill, will you go?

Monday

Tuesday

Wednesday

Thursday

Friday

Saturday

Sunday

NOTHING BETWEEN

Read: Mark 10:17-22

But your iniquities have made a separation between you and your God, And
your sins have hidden His face from you so that He does not hear.
(Isaiah 59:2)

A S I HUNG up the phone, all of the harsh words and accusations I had just spoken
to my brother played back in my mind. My need to be right, to fix things, always
do things my way, caused those unkind words to come out. My brother was the 24/7
caregiver for my mom. A serious fall resulting in the loss of sight in one eye had left her
weak, frail, and fearful. Her hair needed to be washed, and she wouldn't allow us to do
it, so my brother made an appointment to get it taken care of. She refused to go, and he
didn't insist. When I heard about it, I had to speak my mind. After all this was a health
issue. The next morning, I called to apologize for my outburst. I had wounded my brother
when he had been caring for Mom so tenderly and sacrificially. I have felt those times of
tension between myself and others so often, and it always put a wedge in our relationship.
It isn't always what was said. Sometimes it is an action that I took that should have been
avoided or an action that I didn't take that should have been executed.

What have I put between God and myself? For sure it is un-confessed sin. Is it lack
of obedience, time, or just wanting to do my own thing? The list is endless of what I can
put between my Lord and me. Throughout Bible history, there have been others who
struggled with those things that can come between them and God, creating a wedge
in their relationship. Some who come to mind include the rich young ruler and his
possessions, Martha and her busyness, Moses and his fear, David and his lust. Those
things can be insignificant or monumental. Nothing that comes between my Lord and
me is good because it results in a break in communication and fellowship, a wedge in
the relationship.

Prayer:

Father, I don't want anything to come between us. Whatever crowds in, may I quickly confess it and set it right so there is no wedge in our relationship. Amen.

Thought for the Week:

Nothing Between!

At the end of each day, ask the Holy Spirit to reveal anything you have allowed to come between God and yourself.

Monday

Tuesday

Wednesday

Thursday

Friday

Saturday

Sunday

ASSUMPTIONS

Read: 2 kings 5:20-27

But he said to Him, "Lord, with You I am ready to go both to prison and to death!"
(Luke 22:33)

MY HUSBAND IS very attentive to the preparation of details for travel, especially for our travel trailer. Since the batteries are deep cycle for RV use, he assumed (which was very uncharacteristic of him), they were maintenance free, and he didn't check them. The batteries allow us to use the lights and run the pump for water. On a recent outing, we had power the first night. The second night, however, found us playing cards by candlelight with barely enough power to get water.

"I assumed the batteries were maintenance free. What was I thinking? Obviously, I wasn't thinking at all. It came back to bite me!" my husband groaned.

We can assume so many things. How many of us have found ourselves stranded because we assumed we had enough gas to get to the next spot on a long trip or even on our way to work and back? On a deeper level, we often surmise that those around us who are active and serving in church are born again Christians. As parents, we believe that if we bring our children up in a Christian environment, make sure they get to Sunday school, attend youth group, and "walk the talk," that they will choose to follow Jesus and make good decisions.

Living and learning in the right environment doesn't always cause someone to do or say the right things. Peter lived, learned, and walked with Jesus, believing he would stand strong when tested. Then he denied Christ. Although he had done all the right things, his actions did not betray his preparation. Gehazi, Elisha's servant, was with Elisha and saw God's power in the prophecies. He was in the company of the servants of the Lord, and he presumed that since he was with them, he was automatically covered in whatever he did. In his greed, he made a bad choice that resulted in the curse of leprosy upon him.

Because of where and who they were with, Peter and Gehazi were self-deceived. Peter believed he would pass the test, and Gehazi thought it was acceptable to ask for a reward that was not his. As we walk with the Master, we must beware of assuming our relationship with Jesus is acceptable to him simply because we attend church regularly, show up for a Bible study, or serve others. We must always guard against self-deception.

Prayer:

Father God, Am I assuming you are pleased with all I do? When I think I'm okay, show me where I'm not. Amen.

Thought for the Week:

Always check, never assume.

Monday:

Is there a specific area in your relationship with Jesus where you're assuming you're okay? Ask him to show you.

Tuesday:

What area is he showing you in what you assumed you were okay but are not?

Wednesday:

What Scripture verses come to mind that addresses that area?

Thursday:

Is there someone you assumed wasn't a Christian because of his or her appearance?

Friday:

Think of an assumption that turned out to be wrong.

Saturday:

On a lighter level, recall an assumption you made that came back "to bite you."

Sunday:

Besides Peter and Gehazi, find another biblical character who made an assumption that was not true.

PRESSURES

Read: 2 Corinthians 1:8-11

I press on towards the goal for the prize of the upward call of God in Christ Jesus.
(Philippians 3:14)

DO YOU REMEMBER the pressure cooker? Do they still make them? It was a large pot with an airtight lid. Meat and vegetables went into the pot with water, and the lid was secured with a valve on top. After the appropriate time, the pressure was released from the valve, resulting in a meal being cooked in record time. I've heard some horror stories of the steam not being released properly, resulting in a big, messy blow up!

We all seem to be under pressure of one kind or another these days. Tension, just like in a pressure cooker, can build up from many causes. Work deadlines, financial difficulties, strains in relationships, over-commitment are just a few. What matters is how we respond to these points of stress. Hudson Taylor, founder of the China Inland Mission, knew all about pressures of varying degrees. "It doesn't matter, really, how great the pressure is," he used to say; "it only matters *where the pressure lies.* See that it never comes *between* you and the Lord—then, the greater the pressure, the more it presses you to His breast." Paul emphasizes the same point in 2 Corinthians 11:25 and in many other places in his epistles. The many times he faced extreme cold and heat, suffered floggings, stonings, shipwrecks, imprisonment, and hunger to the point of death, those were the times that drove him closer to God.

The decision we must make in every situation of stress and pressure is to discover whether or not it has been sent by God so that we can press closer to his heart. During many of these trying circumstances, we find ourselves doing our own thing. It can also push us to prove we are deserving of a worldly "badge of honor" as we go on and on about how busy and burdened we are. All this results in pushing God away as opposed to drawing closer to him. In 2 Corinthians 1:9 Paul states, "…indeed, we had the sentence of death within ourselves so that we would not trust ourselves, but in God who raises the dead;..." He recognized which pressures were moving him closer to God and which ones were not.

Prayer:

Father God, show me which points of stress I put needlessly on myself. May I willingly accept your pressures as they press me closer to your heart. Amen.

Thought for the Week:

Press me closer, Father.

Each day this week, record a pressure or point of stress. Ask yourself if it drove you closer to God, or further away.

Monday

Tuesday

Wednesday

Thursday

Friday

Saturday

Sunday

RETIREMENT

KEEP ON WALKING

Read: 1 John 1:7

Therefore be imitators of God, as beloved children; and walk in love, just as
Christ also loved you, and gave Himself up for us, an offering and a
sacrifice to God as a fragrant aroma.
(Ephesians 5:1-2)

W HEN YOU REST, you rust," said legendary actress, Helen Hayes. I have arthritis,
not too extreme, but painful enough. I know from reading and doctor advice that
I must keep moving even when it hurts. The body is like a piece of machinery; if idle, it
rusts. Parts lock up and become difficult to move or don't move at all. There does need to
be a balance, and we do need times of rest so as not to burn out physically or emotionally,
but if I have a choice, I would rather burn out than dry up.

A neighbor who recently lost her husband very suddenly walks in the morning
as I do. Every once in a while, we meet somewhere and stop to chat, catching up
on what's going on with our children as they grew up together. The other morning
she confessed to being weary with grieving and caring for her elderly parents and
grandchildren. We both agreed that whatever we are going through, we must keep
on walking.

A spiritual application can always be found in every situation. As I need to keep
walking to keep my joints working, I also need to keep walking in the Spirit moment by
moment, allowing God to keep our relationship working (and my hips). This means I
must also spend time in the Word and time with him. Then I will know his plan for the
day, the details and decisions. I must remember not to run ahead, but to follow, being a
fragrant aroma and offering as I walk with God.

Prayer:

Father God, keep pushing me to walk with you, even when I don't feel like it, physically or spiritually. Amen.

Thought for the Week:

If I am to follow Jesus, I must keep on walking in front (Genesis 17:1), alongside (Galatians 5:16), and behind (2 Corinthians 5:7).

Each morning read the Scriptures above. At the end of each day, record where you followed Jesus either in front of, alongside, or behind.

Monday

Tuesday

Wednesday

Thursday

Friday

Saturday

Sunday

COOKIE ROTATION

Read: Genesis 12:1-4

He changes a wilderness into a pool of water, And a dry land into springs of water; ...
(Psalm 107:35)

WE ARE SUCH creatures of habit! I've been making cookies for over fifty years. When all five children were home, I baked weekly, but now with just the two of us, I don't bake as often. I do find, however, that I'm still going through the recipes in a routine fashion: chocolate chip, oatmeal, molasses, snickerdoodles, and chocolate snappers. I rarely look for something different to try to break out of the cookie rotation.

It seems the older we get, the more of a slave we are to those routines. As the current saying goes, we never "break out of the box." I wonder what opportunities God has for us that we often miss because of our fears or unwillingness to try something new! Especially for those of us that are retired, we need to ask God what his plan is for us to serve him and bring him glory. Using retirement as a permanent vacation is not part of his plan. He has things for us to do, even if our older years are incapacitated in some way. We can count on him to move us out of our cookie cutter routine and into a delicious adventure if we let him.

In his Word, God has provided stories of characters in which he broke into their daily routines and required a complete turnaround from whatever they were doing. Lifestyles and age did not keep God from calling them to do great things.

The Bible records Noah as being six hundred years old when he packed up his sons, wives, and all the animals entering the ark. At age seventy-five, Abram was asked to leave the country he had known, pack his family, livestock, and go. God did not give him a map, he just said he would show him the way. Then he became a father at the age of one hundred. After forty years as a shepherd, Moses was called by God to be a world leader, leading the Jews out of Egypt where they had been slaves for 400 years. Moses was eighty years old when he was obedient to God's call. (He did argue with God, angering the Almighty, but he did go.) These three men were anything but young.

Are we willing to have our routine retirement broken into by God? Maybe God's direction for us is not as earth shattering as it was for Noah, Abram, and Moses, but we should be as obedient and open to whatever he has planned for us! Many of us need to break out of that box we have put ourselves in. There are so many ways we can be used by God because of where we are in life's journey. Careers, training, tests and trials have given us wisdom that God wants to use to bring others to him, which will teach us new things in the process. Now that we are retired, we actually have time for things like volunteering. Crises pregnancy centers always need godly women to counsel. Short-term mission trips give us the opportunity to use a variety of skills in addition to opening our eyes to a new culture and people to experience. Of course, there are always new places and people with whom we can share the Gospel, and even from a sick bed we can pray for others. No matter what our age, God is not finished with us yet.

Prayer:

Father God, life is so exciting with you. I don't want to miss any of it. When you have laid a change on my heart, I pray that I won't argue as Moses did, but instead, go as Abram did. Amen.

Thought for the Week:

Which boxes do I need to break out of?

Thoughts to ponder:

Monday:

Read Genesis 6:13-22 and reflect on Noah's age.

Tuesday:

Consider some areas where you have wanted to volunteer but didn't have the time before.

Wednesday:

Read Genesis 12:4. Has God asked you to move?

Thursday:

If you could go on a short-term mission trip anywhere in the world, where would you want to go?

Friday:

Where is God nudging you to serve?

Saturday:

Ask God to show you an attitude that needs to be changed?

Sunday:

Is there a good thought pattern that needs to become a habit?

SIX SATURDAYS

Read: Genesis 2:2

You will make known to me the path of life;
In Your presence is fullness of joy;
In Your right hand there are pleasures forever.
(Psalm 16:11)

GOD CREATED SEVEN days in our week, six for work and one for rest so we could specifically focus on him. Much has changed in our culture regarding work, rest, and worship. Our worship is all we do every moment of the day. In other words, worship is 24/7. All those years of jobs and raising a family set the schedule for our days and weekends. Going to church on Sundays left Saturdays to get as much done as we could squeeze into them. Home improvement, short trips, and kids' activities filled every Saturday.

Now we are retired from our jobs, and the children are grown and gone. Retirement is like having weeks of nothing but Saturdays! It all sounds so freeing and wonderful, but there are many challenges and changes that we now face. Just waking up in the morning, we are met with decisions we didn't have to make before. Do I want to get up yet? What do I want to do today? Are there certain things that must be done today? We must do a great deal more conscious thinking than we did before. Before we were retired, those decisions were part of our weekly routine, and we didn't have to decide whether or not to get up. Our job or child dictated it.

God tells us to make the most of our time, being always open and obedient to serve when and where God calls (Ephesians 5:15-16). With retirement and our ongoing aging process, there are many changes that we will need to adjust to, allowing God to continue to mature and use us. We need to think outside our predictable box to try new things that will keep us alive, active, and available to be used by God. Even as retired senior citizens, all play and no work will make us dull. As Psalm 16:11 states, God will make known to us the path of life, right on into our senior years, until he takes us home.

Prayer:

Father God, push us on in this new place of retirement in our lives, to embrace with joy every new challenge and change you have for us. Give us willing hearts. Amen.

Thought for the Week:

No emotional or spiritual rocking chair!

If retired, how are you using your six Saturdays? If you are still working, are you allowing yourself to be challenged to do and learn new things?

Monday

Tuesday

Wednesday

Thursday

Friday

Saturday

Sunday

WHAT'S MY EXCUSE?

Read: Psalm 92:12-15

They will still yield fruit in old age;…
(Psalm 92:14a)

I AM A senior citizen! I'm privileged to enjoy discount tickets, have an AARP membership, Medicare, the whole nine yards of perks. Why is it I never thought I would be a senior citizen? The physical part of this aging process is obviously the first part we must deal with: graying hair, wrinkles, health issues. For some reason, we begin to equate that with being "over the hill," useless, not needed, not as capable, and on and on it goes. As usual, we are looking at this from the world's perspective, which is a rather jaundiced view at that. It seems as though we look back to how we looked or what we were doing twenty years ago or so, and think, now what's left? I believe God would shake us to look at his view of where we are, not as the world views us. If God has many years of senior citizenship planned for us, he has work for us to do. I don't think the word *retirement* is in his vocabulary.

There are many saints whose lives speak to us from Scripture who were definitely senior citizens, and God had big plans for them. Moses was eighty when he was called to lead the Israelites out of Egypt. Sarah and Abraham were many, many years past childbearing and parenting when God called them to raise Isaac. Anna was an eighty-four-year-old widow who spent all of her senior years in the temple fasting and praying. Much of David's finest poetry was written after he hung up his sword. The senior woman in the book of Titus is called to teach the younger women. My ninety-four-year-old neighbor isn't jogging any more, but he has published four books since he turned ninety! I think we need to stop looking at the worship of youthfulness in all areas of life and look to God to see what he has planned for us in our senior years, whatever state we may be in physically or otherwise.

Prayer:

Father God, wherever I am in this journey of aging, remind me that you have work for me to do. Open me and fill me with your Holy Spirit, ready to embrace the next adventure with you. Amen.

Thought for the Week:

What's my excuse?

Wait and watch for God's next adventure. Be aware of new things to do, places to go, and things to learn every day.

Monday

Tuesday

Wednesday

Thursday

Friday

Saturday

Sunday

YES, YOU CAN!

Read: Colossians 1:9-12

Therefore, confess your sins to one another, and pray for one another
so that you may be healed. The effective prayer of a righteous man
can accomplish much.
(James 5:16)

WE OFTEN HEAR the lament, sometimes from our loved ones in their senior years, of feeling useless. They may be homebound caring for an ailing mate, fearful of driving, confined to home or a care facility with an illness, or feeling just plain tired. A younger senior citizen may be caring for an elderly parent, feel trapped by the routine, and make good use of time as the one being cared for sleeps.

Because we, as women, and even some men, are doers, we put intercessory prayer far down on our list of ministry priorities. We feel that we are not doing as much as we could because it is not a physical action. It seems much more important to be ministering physically in some way. But the discipline of prayer, intercessory prayer, is so much more challenging spiritually, emotionally, as well as physically. Samuel Shoemaker, in his book, *We Believe in Prayer*, says, "The prayer of intercession means prayer for others. It is our faint echo of Christ's everlasting intercession for us before the Throne of God. It is love and concern for people lifted to the highest point, as we bring them before the Throne of God in prayer." Seniors have experienced so much of life's ups and downs, who better than they to pray for someone specifically because they have "been there."

The story of Job shows us what happens when we pray for others. He lost everything—children, possessions, livestock, and even his health. Chapter 42:10 states, "The Lord restored the fortunes of Job *when* he prayed for his friends, and the Lord increased all that Job had twofold." Interceding for others, in spite of what our circumstances may be, changes our focus from ourselves to others. They are lifted up and so are we to the throne of God. Oswald Chambers says, "Your intercessions can never be mine, and my intercessions can never be yours, but the Holy Spirit makes intercession in our particular lives, without which intercession someone will be impoverished."

Prayer:

Father God, I can always pray. Keep me focused on you, discerning the Holy Spirit's prompting so that no one will be impoverished because of my lack of obedience to pray without ceasing. Amen.

Thought for the Week:

When we can't go, we can go in prayer.
Each day this week, ask God to bring someone to mind that needs your prayers.

Monday

Tuesday

Wednesday

Thursday

Friday

Saturday

Sunday

EXTERNAL LESSONS

DISTRACTIONS

Read John 4:34

I glorified You on earth, having accomplished the work which
You have given Me to do.
(John 17:4)

WE WENT TO a concert for the evening, something we hadn't done for quite a
while. When we got home, we fixed a snack, talked about the concert, and went
to bed. When we came down to the kitchen the next morning, to our horror, there was
no freshly brewed coffee waiting for us. We had been so distracted by our evening out,
we had forgotten to make coffee and set the timer. Worse yet was the fact that we left
the garage door open all night!

Another time, I burned cookies because I went off to use that fifteen-minute baking
time to do another task. They were distractions and although not serious, they were still
distractions. Sometimes I am so overloaded with ideas, thoughts, and plans of what to
do next, that nothing is completed, or I just forget the priority in which they need to be
accomplished.

I don't think this is just a problem for seniors. Today's lifestyle is one of much stress
and busyness that fills every possible minute with accomplishments, and whether big or
small, we rush from one thing to another as if it was all ordained by God!

Oswald Chambers said, "It is extraordinary what an enormous power there is in
simple things to distract our attention from God." God definitely wants our attention
all of the time. The things of the world are constantly pulling us away, whispering or
shouting for our attention. I can walk away from my quiet time with the Lord and a
specific person he has impressed upon me to call, and then promptly be distracted by
unimportant household tasks. I may make a note to myself and look at it several times
during the day, but still never do it. The list of subtle and not so subtle things that distract
us is long—television, shopping, the Internet, books, and activities of all sorts. Jesus was

never distracted. He was never in a hurry. He accomplished what his Father gave him to do. We need to follow his example.

Prayer:

Father God, I confess my weakness to be so easily distracted. Strengthen my focus on you, your Word, and on what you have called me to do next. May I be like Jesus and "accomplish what you have called me to do." Amen.

Thought for the Week:

A distraction can be fatal!
What simple, daily distraction pulled you away from God? What did it teach you?

Monday

Tuesday

Wednesday

Thursday

Friday

Saturday

Sunday

SUCKED IN

Read: Ephesians 6:12

Be of sober spirit, be on the alert. Your adversary, the devil, prowls around
like a roaring lion, seeking someone to devour."
(1 Peter 5:8)

AS CHRISTIANS, WE all know the enemy of our soul is unseen. Satan is a deceiver, a
liar, deceptive and subtle in all his ways. There are so many ways in which he snares
us, ways that are not bad, or evil in themselves, but not what God had in mind.

Recently I have been shocked into awareness by one of those ploys of Satan. I had
been sucked into watching too much television. The pull is sometimes so strong that just
walking into a room with the television on grabs and holds my attention. Not long ago, I
hardly watched any at all, and if I did, it was a specific show or special feature. Part of the
infrequency of viewing was a time issue. A house full of children, my returning to school,
homework, and not having the hundreds of extra channels made it easy to ignore the
"box." In addition, we only had one television in our basement family room, which meant
a conscious choice had to be made. I know friends who have a television in every room!

We have recently downsized into a smaller home now that it is just the two of us. The
television is in part of the great room/kitchen area. If my husband wants to watch a program
that I'm not interested in, I need to find another room and close the door. The trap comes
when we just watch to watch, flipping channels, rather than just turning it off. When we do
watch a car race or ball game, something very subtle happens when it is over. We continue
to watch even though we are not really interested. We've been sucked in. I've also notice
that something physical happens, as well as the mental shut-off. My body becomes more
lethargic. I jokingly say, I've gone from a couch potato to couch potato puree.

Television is not the only thing that can suck us in to wasting time. The Internet is
a great technological tool for research and finding answers to many questions, but that
too can suck us into spending hours and hours of searching for information that is not
really needed. E-mailing and constantly checking e-mail is another trap. Talking on cell

phones has really gotten out of hand too. I think the next generation is going to be born with a phone for one of their ears. How do we rationalize hours spent doing Sudoku? If we ask the Father, I'm sure he will show us other places in our lives where we waste God's gift of time. "All things are lawful, but not all things are profitable. All things are lawful, but not all things edify" (1 Corinthians 10:23).

I know God does not want hours wasted, no matter how we rationalize the time. We can learn and benefit from many programs on television as well as just enjoying a show that is entertaining. We also know that a great deal of television these days is very immoral and violent. Most of these hours spent on television, the Internet, cell phone use, etc., could be used in a much more beneficial way. Spending time in the Word, encouraging someone with a phone call or visit, taking a prayer walk, or just finding a silent place to commune with God would be more profitable to us and bring glory to God.

Prayer:

Father, forgive me for wasting many precious hours that I could have spent in the Word or communing with you. To thwart Satan's ploy, speak to me when television viewing, or doing anything else that has taken your place and your plan for the way my time should be spent. Remind me that I have the power to stop wasting time. Amen

Thought for the Week:

"Little children, guard yourselves from idols" (1 John 5:21).

At the end of each day this week, recall a time spent wasting time. How could you have used those minutes or hours in a way more pleasing to the Father?

Monday

Tuesday

Wednesday

Thursday

Friday

Saturday

Sunday

DROWNING IN STUFF

Read: 2 Corinthians 9:8

Then He said to them, "Beware, and be on your guard against every form of greed;
for not even when one has an abundance does his life consist of his possessions."
(Luke 12:15)

WHEN WE THINK of drowning, we think of water. Smothering brings forth an image of a pillow over our face, but possessions have a way of accomplishing the same thing. We have recently downsized to a significantly smaller house. After thirty years in one house in which we raised five kids, you can imagine all the stuff we had accumulated. In this day and age, we all seem to be drowning or we are being suffocated by things. They have possessed us. The irony of it all is our focus on "more" and "wants" while at the same time bemoaning what we need to get rid of, throw out, sell, or give away. What madness we get ourselves into. The vicious cycle is the store to the garage sale and then back again to the store to buy something that will be in next year's garage sale. Glyn Evans says, "When I can no longer use something, I must give it to someone who can. Jesus was the great 'giver-upper' When he died, he owned nothing. The world is always telling me what I need; and if I listen to such talk, I will accumulate forever and yet never find satisfaction" (*Daily With the King*).

A more subtle, but harmful possessiveness can be with those we love. I can well remember many years ago an incident where God showed me how possessive I was of our youngest child, Rob, who was then one year old. Our dream trip to Europe was a reality, the date for departure was set. The night before we were to leave, Rob came down with croup! He never had respiratory problems before and hasn't since. Our friend who was to care for him while we were gone, told us not to worry, and we did trust her completely. But my heart cried out, "Lord, how can I leave him?" To this day, I can clearly hear the Lord say to me, "You're holding him too tight. He's not yours; he's mine. Let go, trust me." We went and Rob was fine.

Now that all the children are grown and gone, I find myself sometimes responding in the same way with my husband. I hold him too tight. I get angry when a health issue arises, fearing a heart attack, stroke, or whatever might take him from me. Then the Lord reminds me of the incident with Rob and also the Abraham and Isaac story. God never tests us on what we hate, but on what we love. That keeps us from being abandoned to him. Possessions, and even a loved one, can become a possession that takes the place of God.

Prayer:

Father, speak to my heart and reveal those things and loved ones that possess me, keeping me from total surrender to you. Amen

Thought for the Week:

Let go!
Every day ask God to bring to mind someone or something you need to let go of and why.

Monday

Tuesday

Wednesday

Thursday

Friday

Saturday

Sunday

THE TREE BRANCH

Read Isaiah 58:10-12

And the Lord will continually guide you, And satisfy your desire in scorched places,
And give strength to your bones; And you will be like a watered garden, And
like a spring of water whose waters do not fail.
(Isaiah 58:11)

WE HAD SUFFERED a few years of drought, always forgetting during the dry winter months to water our large trees. This year we had a glorious spring, everything blooming early with breathtaking beauty. The days were unusually warm with very few cold snaps of rain and snow, but there is a great deal of wind in our area, and this year more than usual, or so it seemed.

One evening as we were eating dinner, my husband looked out the window and exclaimed, "A huge branch just broke off the big poplar!" We were surprised, because it was a good-sized branch fully green with many leaves. It is normally the dead branches that come down in the wind. Upon cutting it up, we discovered a very dry branch, with no moisture inside. It was very easy to break the smaller branches and saw the larger ones into small chunks.

As we were snapping and sawing this very healthy looking branch into wood for the fire, the Lord reminded me of how my appearance is so important to me. I spend too much time, not to mention money, concerned over hair, clothes, etc., for my outward appearance, while neglecting to nourish and water my soul. During those dry winter seasons of life's journey, I need to be "watering" the inside with the Word, prayer, and time spent with the Lord. When the "winds" come, I will be strengthened to withstand whatever blows my way.

Prayer:

Father, every time this child of yours looks in the mirror to check on the outward appearance, speak to my heart. Show me what I look like on the inside and what needs "watering." Amen

Thought for the Week:

I may look "healthy" on the outside, but on inside there may be "dry bones." Ask God to reveal to you those dry areas that need "watering."

Monday

Tuesday

Wednesday

Thursday

Friday

Saturday

Sunday

R.W.T.

Read: Psalm 37:5-7

Wait for the Lord; Be strong and let your heart take courage;
Yes, wait for the Lord.
(Psalm 27:14)

A FEW YEARS ago, a close friend went through a difficult time. She was in the middle of a conflict and in some ways, was being persecuted for her stand in what and how she believed the Lord was leading her. What made this particularly hard about this conflict was in the body of believers. As her listening ear and prayer warrior, I would e-mail R.W.T. to her as encouragement—REST, WAIT, TRUST. All three of these very significant action verbs proliferate the pages of Scripture, especially in the Psalms. I believe most of us have difficulty doing all three.

REST Is this an action verb? Yes, I believe it is. We think of rest in terms of inactivity, such as taking a nap, but what this really means is the action of mentally placing the circumstances of the present struggle firmly on the Lord by, "…casting all your anxiety on Him, because He cares for you" (1 Peter 5:7). In Psalm 37:7, David is telling his listeners to rest in the Lord and to not fret in the midst of difficult circumstances.

WAIT This is even a more burdensome command to obey. We, at least some of us, are so impatient for God to work it out, but the Bible says, "Rest in the Lord and wait patiently for Him" (Psalm 37:7). God tells us twice to wait, take courage, be strong and wait in Psalm 27:14, and verse 13 tells us what happens if we don't wait for Him, "I would have despaired …in the land of the living."

TRUST "Trust also in Him and He will do it" (Psalm 37:5). More times than not we take things into our own hands, rather than trusting the only one who can work it out. Trust, and its various forms, is used numerous times throughout Scripture as God encourages his children to trust him. I think God is making a point! He is trustworthy. Whom else can we trust, but the Creator of all? My dear friend, did R.W.T. It was a struggle to do those action verbs of mental and spiritual ascent. It took time, but God worked it out according to his plan because she RESTED, WAITED, and TRUSTED in him to do it.

Prayer:

Father, when I want to run ahead of you and "fix" what I think is broken in rash words and actions, speak loudly to me to R.W.T.! Amen

Thought for the Week:

Rest, Wait, Trust.
Is there now a difficulty that brings you to practice R.W.T.?

Monday

Tuesday

Wednesday

Thursday

Friday

Saturday

Sunday

SEND, SUSTAIN, SEVER

Read: John 20:21; Psalm 119:116; Ezekiel 36:26

Lord, send me anywhere, but go with me. Lay any burden
on me, only sustain me. Sever any tie,
but the tie that binds me to Thy self.
David Livingstone

DAVID LIVINGSTONE, A nineteenth century missionary from Scotland, gave his life to making Jesus known in Africa. Like Livingstone, the prophet Isaiah heard the voice of the Lord asking who will go for us. Isaiah boldly declares, "Here am I. Send me" (Isaiah 6:8). He is then commissioned by the Lord as a prophet and directed to what he should say.

Many have heard the call of God and immediately respond. To bring it to where we live today is no different for us, individually, as it was for Isaiah. When the Lord asks, "Who will go for us?" our response should always be, "Here am I. Send me." As David Livingstone said, "Send me anywhere, only go with me." The Lord promises to never leave us or forsake us, no matter where he has sent us or how awful the circumstances.

The biography of Brother Yun, *The Heavenly Man,* by Paul Hattaway, gives a startling picture of a man who suffered prolonged torture and imprisonments for his faith. His account emphatically states that the Lord never forsook or left him through it all. There are many places God sends us today that may or may not be as dramatic, but are still important. It may be a battlefield, visiting the shut-ins, helping a neighbor, or serving in a specific capacity at church. When we respond that we will go, he will go with us (Joshua 1:9).

Livingstone then said to put any burden on me, only sustain me. One is reminded of the Apostle Paul's thorn in the flesh and how the Lord said his grace was sufficient to bear it. Paul was sustained through the burdens of flogging, shipwrecks, stonings, and many other dangers. We know we all will have trials, tests, and sufferings in this life, and God promises to sustain us through them or take us home. Our burdens today may be like that of Paul or other missionaries in dangerous places, but most of us will face burdens such as caring for a parent or a spouse who is bedridden, heartaches and concerns for a wayward child, or a broken relationship. "Cast your burden upon the Lord, and He will sustain you; He will never allow the righteous to be shaken" (Psalm 55:22).

Livingstone then asked God to "sever any tie, but the tie that binds me to thyself." This is the hardest place for us. We go, he is sustaining us through whatever, but then God gets really personal and expects us to remove those things in our lives that keep us from following him completely, surrendering *all*. Often it is our prejudices and biases. It could be an unhealthy relationship or those possessions that strangle us. When the Holy Spirit reveals ties to other things, we need to ask God to do surgery and cut them out of our life immediately (Matthew 5:30). When one of those ties has been removed, we need to ask God to fill that empty place with more of him. He will do as he has promised.

Prayer:

Father God, I will go, sustain me always, but most importantly, sever any tie except the one that connects me to you. Amen.

Thought for the Week:

Sever what is not of you.

Each day this week, ask God to show you what you need to sever that comes between you and him. It could be something seemingly trivial or more monumental.

Monday

Tuesday

Wednesday

Thursday

Friday

Saturday

Sunday

HOLIDAYS

THANKS, GOD!

Read: Colossians 1:16-20

Thanks be to God for His indescribable gift!
(2 Corinthians 9:15)

SEVERAL YEARS AGO, a dear friend gave me a cute figurine of a lamb. He has a bell on a ribbon around his neck and he is rather fat with his wool needing to be sheared. I kept him on the coffee table for several years as a constant reminder to myself that, "All of us like sheep have gone astray, each of us has turned to his own way;…" (Isaiah 53:6). It is amazing to me how easily we can go astray.

I remember a time when I knew I was doing too much: school, singing in various choirs, Bible study, besides being wife and mother. I had gone astray because my heart was not right. I was going through the motions, with no personal relationship with my Father. I would sit in church or a Bible study, my focus lost in a fog of too many diversions. Thankfully, God brought just the right test to wake me up from my drifting.

Recently I moved the lamb to the mantle beneath a very rugged painting of Jesus praying. It is finger painted on a weathered board, in sepia tones. The other morning, during my quiet time, I glanced up at that painting as I often do. It was a startling thought when I realized the significance of that lamb I had placed there beneath the painting. The lamb can represent us, but it also represents him for us. He is the lamb that was slain, taking away the sins of the world, my sin, my going astray. There are times, as was this moment, when the realization of just what Jesus did for me, hits home once again, and I am awed into silence. Everything *is* because of Jesus as the lamb—forgiveness, healing, rest, peace, and life itself. There is no fullness of life here or eternal life there without the blood of the lamb.

We know that every day is Thanksgiving because of what God through Jesus did for us, "…and through Him to reconcile all things to Himself, having made peace through the blood of His cross;…" (Colossians 1:20a).

Prayer:

Thank you Father, for the gift of your Son. Constantly remind me of what he has done for me. Startle me out of my complacency. May my heart be forever grateful. Amen.

Thought for the Week:

Give thanks with a grateful heart.
Each evening this week, thank God for something you take for granted.

Monday

Tuesday

Wednesday

Thursday

Friday

Saturday

Sunday

CHRISTMAS?

Read: John 1:1-5

And the Word became flesh, and dwelt among us, and we saw His glory,
glory as of the only begotten from the Father,
full of grace and truth.
(John 1:14)

WHAT WOULD HAPPEN if I, as a Christian, would truly celebrate Christ's birth and the significance of this event? What would happen deep in my innermost being if there were no gatherings of family and friends around festive food, or lights in proliferation everywhere, no trees, no decorations, no gifts, no cards, no pageants or musical presentations in churches? Would I still be as excited, filled with all those uplifting warm fuzzies I usually feel this time of year? Or would I be depressed and joyless without all those worldly, outward trappings?

What would happen if I went into a darkened church on Christmas Eve or Christmas Day with no services planned; only silence, with no music or spoken word? Would I be able to worship the Christ child here or anywhere, for that matter, without the visible, audio stuff?

Isn't that how I am to celebrate Christmas, in silent awe, on my knees, worshipping God becoming flesh—Jesus—Emmanuel—God with us?

Prayer:

Father God, may I never celebrate your Son's birth in the worldly trappings. May his birth be fresh each year in the wonder and amazement of the cross to come. Amen.

Thought for the Week:

What have I done to Christmas?

Each day leading up to Christmas, ask yourself what is there in the decorations you use, the music you listen to, and the programs you attend that speaks of God becoming man and bringing Him glory.

Monday

Tuesday

Wednesday

Thursday

Friday

Saturday

Sunday

WE ALMOST MISSED!

Read: Psalm 127:3

Thanks be to God for His indescribable gift!
(2 Corinthians 9:15)

TWENTY-SEVEN YEARS AGO, we almost missed accepting a gift that has blessed our lives and the lives of many others. At this time, we had been foster parents and had loved and cared for many children, mostly toddlers and infants. When a call came for a much needed home for one of these little ones, there was never time to pray to ask God for direction. We had to depend upon a prompting by the Holy Spirit. When the call came twenty-seven years ago for a four-week old infant who had been close to death because of neglect, I just felt I wasn't ready for another one at that time. I was tired. But this time, we had the night to pray so we could give our decision in the morning. We almost said no, but we are so very thankful we said yes to God and this child.

Rob became our own, and from the very first moment he was placed in my arms, he has blessed our family and so many others. He is now married and is trained to be a paramedic. His quiet, sensitive, tender spirit will continue to be used by God to help others. It is hard to believe that we almost missed accepting this gift from God!

Christmas is over and once again, the season brings God's gift of Jesus as a baby to accept or reject. We pray that this Christmas was for many the time to accept God's gift of his Son. We know that not only did this baby change and bless our lives twenty-seven years ago, but also God's Son continues to change and bless our lives forever.

Prayer:

Father God, I thank you for the prompting of the Holy Spirit in my life. I thank you for speaking to my heart to say yes to this baby, but most of all, for saying yes to your Son, Jesus. Amen.

Thought for the Week:
Say yes to the gift of Jesus!
Have you truly accepted the gift of Jesus, or are you still trying to earn it?

Monday

Tuesday

Wednesday

Thursday

Friday

Saturday

Sunday

SANTA TO BUNNY?

Read: Galatians 2:20

For I determined to know nothing among you except
Jesus Christ, and Him crucified.
(1 Corinthians 2:2)

CHRISTMAS WAS TYPICAL for us this year, no snow, but we did have snow for Easter in mid-April. A typical Easter as a child meant new clothes, a dress, hat, shoes, purse, and gloves. We always went to church, but the real excitement was what the Easter bunny would leave in a basket by our beds the night before. (I hate using *Easter* and *bunny* in the same sentence now.) Even beyond the surprises from the Easter bunny was the Easter egg hunt at my aunt's house in the afternoon. She was very artistic and painted baskets of eggs for us to hunt. She always went all out for all the holidays for her nieces and nephews. Somewhere in all the Easter fluff, however, I knew what Easter was all about. I loved the story of Jesus rising from the dead. I knew he had done it all for me.

Now, many years later, I stand in a store surrounded by the commercial Easter. Every year, remnants of the Valentine cards and heart shaped boxes of candy, shamrocks and leprechauns, are on a sale table marked 75 percent off to make way for baskets, pastel colored candy and eggs, fluffy chickens and bunnies, and even chocolate crosses! Every year the commercialism gets bigger and starts earlier. As Christians, we still get sucked in, whether for our children or grandchildren.

Where are you in all this Jesus? After all, it's my responsibility to keep my focus on Jesus. If Easter becomes matter-of-fact and I am caught up in colored eggs and fluffy stuffed animals, it is my fault. What is my part in changing the world's view of Easter? Besides not purchasing the Easter stuff, I can send cards to family and friends proclaiming the resurrection and all that Jesus has done for us. Inviting family and friends to Easter services is important, but I must always proclaim Easter for what it really is in the way I live every day. This, too, is my responsibility as Peter states in 1 Peter 1:18-19, "…

knowing that you were not redeemed with perishable things like silver and gold from your futile way of life inherited from your forefathers, but with the precious blood, as of a lamb unblemished and spotless, the blood of Christ." The hope that is in me because of the resurrection must shine through me touching the lives of those who go from Santa to bunny, to bring them to the manger, then to the cross.

Prayer:

Father, keep me from buying into the Santa/bunny focus. May I focus from the manger to the cross to the celebration of what you have done for me. Amen.

Thought for the Week:

Just give me Jesus!
What worldly trappings keep you from celebrating the risen Christ?

Monday

Tuesday

Wednesday

Thursday

Friday

Saturday

Sunday

HEART LESSONS

WHAT A DIFFERENCE!

Read: Titus 3:5-7

…but if we walk in the light as He Himself is in the Light, we have fellowship
with one another, and the blood of Jesus his Son cleanses us from all sin.
(1 John 1:7)

THERE IS AN old song from the 30s and 40s with the first line stating, "What a
difference a day makes, twenty-four little hours." Recently, I was singing that song
substituting the word shower for day. Foot surgery made a shower impossible for the first
two weeks of recovery. Sponge baths just don't cut it! When I could finally bathe from
head to toe all at once, what a difference it made! I finally felt clean.

Water, our most precious commodity, quenches our thirst as well as cleans everything
from head to toe, plus our clothes, cars, and most everything. The pictures God paints
for us using water, symbolically and literally, are numerous. In Old Testament times, the
priests' washing was an outward symbol of purification. This ritual of washing had to
be done before they could minister as priest. A guest invited to your house would have
his feet washed upon entering. After God brought the people of Israel back from all the
nations to their own land, the prophet Ezekiel was given a word from God to relay to
them, "Then I will sprinkle clean water on you, and you will be clean; I will cleanse you
from all your filthiness and from all your idols" (Ezekiel 36:25). In Psalm 51:2, after David
had been confronted with his sin with Bathsheba, he confessed and repented praying,
"Wash me thoroughly from my iniquity, and cleanse me from my sin." The physical
washing mirrored the spiritual cleansing.

In the New Testament, we read of Jesus being baptized by John. For Jesus this was the
beginning of his earthly ministry. Baptism for Christians, by sprinkling or submersion, is
the physical action taken to identify and say to everyone that they belong to Christ. This
is also the outward picture of our sins being washed away because of Christ taking them
upon himself on the cross. We are washed by the Word as Jesus tells us in John 15:3,
"You are already clean because of the word which I have spoken to you." In 1 John 1:9 it

says, "If we confess our sins, He is faithful and just to forgive us our sins and to cleanse us from all unrighteousness." The Old Testament law said that without the shedding of blood there could be no forgiveness (Hebrews 9:22). But now, because of the shed blood on the cross, we are forgiven and washed clean!

Prayer:

Father God, water and blood—may they always be significant to me as they mean that I can be washed clean from sin and be forgiven always. Amen.

Thought for the Week:

"What can take away my sin? Nothing but the blood of Jesus." Robert Lowry
What difference has the shed blood of Jesus meant in your daily walk?

Monday

Tuesday

Wednesday

Thursday

Friday

Saturday

Sunday

TURN UP THE HEAT!

Read: Proverbs 17:3

Behold, I have refined you, but not as silver;
I have tested you in the furnace of affliction.
(Isaiah 48:10)

I FEEL FORTUNATE to live in an area of the country that has four distinct seasons. Well, maybe that's not quite accurate. Spring in the Sierra Nevada's might not quite come into focus when there is snow on the blossoms, if we even have blossoms! This year, for instance, all of the spring vegetation that begins in late February and continues into May happened all in the first two weeks of May, and then it snowed! But every once in a while we do have a beautiful spring that looks just like the pictures in books with the delicate pastels of blossoms and the new green leaves. Everything seems to burst into life from crisp, fresh mornings, warming up to hot days.

Speaking of hot days, we can have several days and/or weeks of one hundred plus degree-days, which tests our attitude towards everything. Just getting into the car after a short errand sends us panting until the air conditioning is going full blast, if you are blessed to have air conditioning. Some thrive in this kind of heat. Me, I begin a slow melt down after about eighty degrees. All my energy and enthusiasm for anything just evaporates and all that is left is a withered me with a grumpy, whiny attitude. Is there a lesson here about attitude when it is 103 degrees outside and this heat is unbearably oppressive?

There are times when God tests us through physical things like unbearably hot, summer days. But he can and does also turn up the heat in places in our character that needs refining or eliminating too.

The other morning in the car at eight A.M. when I was already feeling like I was being burned alive, I asked God, "What area of my life are you zeroing in on? Show me quick, no slow burn, I want the fire out now!" I could almost hear God chuckle as he told me those impurities in me can sometimes be burned out in a flash, but most of the time it takes a slow burn with him turning up the heat until the job is done. His refiner's fire is not for silver, nor the furnace for the gold, but for me and all the impurities that need to be burned out. As it says in Proverbs 17:3, the Lord is testing my heart and he will turn up the heat until all impurities are gone.

Prayer:

Father, I hate the heat, both physical and spiritual. Help me to understand why the heat and testing of my attitudes is a lifelong process. May I cooperate with you as you turn up the heat. Amen.

Thought for the Week:

Turn Up the Heat, God!
Did you feel God's heat this week? What was the incident?

MARTHA-ITIS

Read: John 11:17-29

But the Lord answered and said to her, "Martha, Martha, you are worried and bothered about so many things; but only one thing is necessary, for Mary has chosen the good part, which shall not be taken away from her."
(Luke 10:41-42)

AFTER BREAKFAST, STILL in pajamas, I can find much to do besides cleaning up the breakfast dishes. A cupboard may need straightening, a refrigerator drawer may need attention, all while being aware that this is supposed to be my quiet time. At a dinner party, I have no trouble preparing or serving, but then I am anxious to move everyone into the living room so I can load the dishwasher. I hate to admit it, but I look forward to when everyone leaves, not that I don't enjoy their company, but because I desire to finish the cleanup, fully aware that I need to visit with my guests. I have a bad case of "Martha-itis."

"Martha, Martha," Jesus says. I hear him saying that a lot to me, slowing me down and inviting me to sit at his feet. There is a book I saw in the bookstore with the title, *Having a Mary Heart in a Martha World*. My title would be *Having a Martha Heart, but Needing a Mary Heart in the World*. He is working in me to bring me to a closer place of balance, a split personality, half Mary and half Martha. When I search the Word for more places where Martha is mentioned, I find the indication given that she found that balance. When their brother died, and they were in mourning but heard Jesus was coming, it was Martha that took action and went to meet him while Mary sat in the house (John 11:20). The Scripture further tells us that as Jesus questioned Martha, the encounter revealed her belief in him as the Christ. She obviously had listened to his teaching with a devoted, receptive heart. In John 12:1-2, Martha is once again serving, but this time Jesus does not question her motivation for doing so.

As Christians, we know that there is a necessary balance in all areas of our lives. Those of us with cases of Martha-itis of varying degrees need to come away and sit at his feet and listen. He will tell us when, where and how. He has created us to be who we are, whether a Mary or a Martha, and whichever personality is stronger needs the balance of the other.

Prayer:

Father, you created me as a Martha. Show me when my Martha personality pulls me away from you. Help me to listen so I know when I am "to sit" and when I am "to do." Amen.

Thought for the Week:

We all need the Mary and Martha split personality.

At the end of each day this week, record whether you were more of a Martha or a Mary.

Monday

Tuesday

Wednesday

Thursday

Friday

Saturday

Sunday

THREE CHOICES

Read: Joshua 24:15

But may it never be that I would boast, except in the cross
of our Lord, Jesus Christ...
(Galatians 6:14a)

THE NUMBER THREE is very significant whenever it is used in the Bible, the most important being the Father, Son and Holy Spirit. Jesus said that after his crucifixion he would rise three days later. The Apostle Peter denied Christ three times. Jesus asked Peter three times "Do you love me?" and then told him to "Feed my sheep" three times. Paul also encountered the number three after his conversion, as he was blind for three days. Paul was stoned, shipwrecked, and beaten with rods three times. He asked the Lord to take away the thorn in his flesh three times. There are many more places in Scripture where the number three is important.

As Christians, the number three is also significant for us today. We all have three choices to make on a daily basis, all of them having consequences. We must decide whether or not to live for self, to follow in the world's system, or to live for Christ. In each moment of time, it is either me, them, or him.

We like to think and verbally claim that we live for Christ, but in reality, first of all, we live for self. When a call comes to help someone in some way, the initial response is whether or not we want to do it. We might have doubts as to whether or not we can handle the situation or just a fear of the unknown. It could be just that we are selfish with our time. Self gets in the way of a great deal that God wants to teach us and do through us. He is adequate for whatever he has called us to do.

Our second choice is to be a worldly Christian. That's when we become great fence-straddlers. We are so influenced by the world and the culture we live in that often the action to fit in, make a good impression, choose the momentary pleasure, or purchase the unneeded item becomes living in the world. The choices we make on the fence never even give God a thought. He may, and most likely does, have something far better for us. Every time we are on the fence, we are in no man's land and certainly not in God's territory.

Our third choice is really the only choice. To live for Christ opens us up to living life to the fullest. It is not easy, and many just throw up their hands and say it is impossible. But with Christ and the Holy Spirit's empowering all things are possible. To live for Christ means we focus everything we do in the light of him and his plan.

Prayer:

Father God, the choice is really easy. I want to live for you, but sometimes I know I don't. When it comes to that moment of decision, strengthen me to pick you and your plan in every situation. Amen.

Thought for the Week:

It is either me, them or God!

At the end of each day this week, recall when you made a conscious choice to choose God over yourself or the world.

Monday

Tuesday

Wednesday

Thursday

Friday

Saturday

Sunday

ME, MYSELF, AND I

Read: 2 Timothy 3:1-5

For men will be lovers of self,…
(2 Timothy 3:2a)

RICK WARREN'S, *THE Purpose Driven Life* opens this way: "It's not about you." This statement is, for me, the bottom line of all my conflicts. I do love God with all my mind, soul, and spirit, or at least I am being brought to that as God works with me to make me more like Christ. But it's during the present day-by-day times where the battle plays out. Why is it I can't die to self? Why are my first thoughts to ask me-centered questions when God has impressed upon me a specific thing to do? What is it going to cost me? Is it going to be fun? Will I be bored? Will it be painful? Will others be impressed by my sacrifice? How unpleasant will this task be? On and on it goes. It is all very discouraging to me that after all these years of walking with the Lord, that I'm still so very self-centered.

We know others, including heroes of the Bible, who have walked closely with God yet struggled with the same issues. Moses responded to God's call with excuses. Sarah and Abraham took matters into their own hands. The rich young ruler could not part with his money. In contrast to this, there are others who, for the most part, never thought of themselves. Ruth stands out as an exemplary example of selflessness. Her husband, brother-in-law, and father-in-law had died. Naomi, her mother-in-law, a foreigner to Ruth's homeland, decided to return to her own people. She urged Ruth to stay with her people, but Ruth returned with Naomi to her country. I don't know about you, but if my husband died, I would want to stay with people of my own religion and culture, not travel to live among a strange people and religion. I would want all the comfort I could get. It would be all about me!

Oswald Chambers says in *My Utmost for His Highest,* "Beware of any belief that makes you self indulgent; it came from the pit, no matter how beautiful it sounds." That sound is the voice of the enemy that whispers, "It's your right and you deserve it." How much better to hear the Master say, "Well done, good and faithful servant."

Prayer:

Father God, when you call me to whatever you would have me do, may I remember that it's not about me but all about you. Amen.

Thought for the Week:

It's not about me—ever.

Each day this week, record when you put yourself first either in thought, word, or deed.

Monday

Tuesday

Wednesday

Thursday

Friday

Saturday

Sunday

INDIFFERENCE

Read: John 13:33-34

Beloved, if God so loved us, we also ought to love one another.
(I John 4:11)

INDIFFERENCE. WHAT A cold, empty word. A shivering nothing. It is a word reflecting no emotion or feeling. It shows an attitude of "whatever" or "I couldn't care less." It exposes a heart void of passion and compassion. It is intriguing how many words stand in contrast to one another. Love and hate are two of those words and both evoke emotion.

In our home Bible study, we are studying 1 John. In both his gospel and his first epistle, John uses many contrasts, one of them being love and hate. He uses love with the meaning of *agape*, which differs from the love of warm feeling and emotions. Agape love is a purposeful attitude to respect another child of God. It is a selfless love, to put that person above you, desiring to do good for them. John says we are to love one another numerous times in 1 John. He says, "Little children, let us not love with word or tongue, but in deed and truth" (I John 3:18). This shows that love must be active. We often think of love's opposite, hate, being expressed in strong words and actions. Do we claim that we don't hate anybody? But do we agape our brothers and sisters in Christ? Or are we indifferent towards them? Do we ignore and avoid those whose personalities clash with ours? What about people who are just plain irritating? What about people who use us? Or those who just can't seem to get their act together? When caller ID shows who is calling, and it is one of "those calls," do we answer the phone?

Indifference shows total disregard for the other person as a child of God, or one who might become his child. Ignoring, avoiding, or not caring about a fellow believer is a form of hate and hurts the person just the same. A quote from an old novel seems to sum it up. "I had not known that love was obedience. You want to love and you can't, and all the time love is not some marvelous thing you feel but some hard thing you do. And this in a way is easier because with God's help you can command your will when you can't command your feelings. With us feelings seem to be important, but He doesn't appear to agree with us" (*The Scent of Water*, by Elizabeth Goudge).

"A new commandment I give to you, that you love one another, even as I have loved you, that you also love one another" (John 13:34). Obedience to the command of Jesus is what is required of us. If we love God and abide in him, we have his spirit. His love will flow from us, not only to fellow believers, but also to those who don't know how much God loves them and desires them to become his children.

Prayer:

Father God, it sounds so easy to love one another, but I know it is hard to love as you command. I ask for you to bring to my immediate attention the first moment that attitude of indifference creeps in. May I confess immediately and ask to be filled by the Spirit with your unconditional love. Amen.

Thought for the Day (and Every Day):

Love one another.

Each day ask yourself if there was an incident when you were indifferent in thought, word, or deed. Confess and ask for forgiveness. Is there something you can do to make it right?

Monday

Tuesday

Wednesday

Thursday

Friday

Saturday

Sunday

SELF-SUFFICIENCY

Read: 1 Corinthians 12:12-26

For the body is not one member, but many.
(1 Corinthians 12:14)

WE ALL KNOW at least one of those "control freaks," but generally don't consider ourselves to be one. Oh, how we dislike not being in control. We sing the song, "All to Jesus I Surrender" with much fervor, not realizing how little we do surrender or relinquish control to God. Our cultural attitudes play a big part in this, as we are encouraged to be self-sufficient, independent, in control, and a productive member of society. We don't want to be leaches on anyone or society.

In our human relationships, God did not intend for us to go it alone. He created Eve for Adam, and he gives us a spouse, family, friends and co-workers. Working and living together, we support one another using the gifts God has given us. In 1 Corinthians 12, Paul gives us an analogy of how we are to function with one another. He uses our bodies as an illustration about how all the parts fit and work together, each one being important.

When we are, or think we are, self-sufficient, we are also self-centered, self-absorbed, and selfish. This also has its roots in pride. We find out being in control is a lonely place to be. Our relationships with each other are shallow and only on the surface. We get to know one another on a deeper level when we work together at home, at work, and in ministry. We really do need each other, and that is the way God created us.

Another problem with being in control results in not allowing others to function in their gifts. When we try to do it all, others are cheated out of serving and learning. Those of us that tend to be in control rush ahead and do tasks insuring that they will get done. Most of the time, we do these tasks without God involved at all. He may have had someone in mind for that specific job to benefit him or her in some way, and we just took over. As a parent, there were times when teaching a child a specific chore frustrated me, because it wasn't done to my liking. I would either do it myself, or redo what the child had done. I did not give them the opportunity to learn, succeed, or fail. Father, forgive me.

Prayer:

Father God, take the self out of everything. I really do not want to be in control and self-sufficient. You do a much better job. Amen.

Thought for the Week:

"The most precarious thing is to try and live without God." Oswald Chambers
What did you leave God out of today?

Monday

Tuesday

Wednesday

Thursday

Friday

Saturday

Sunday

ROAD WORK AHEAD

Read: Philippians 3:12-14

...for it is God who is at work in you,
both to will and to work for His good pleasure.
(Philippians 2:13)

WE HAVE A saying where I live: "Reno has two seasons, winter and road construction!" The last few years have seen those orange cones and signs in proliferation. A trench for the train to pass through the center of town unhindered kept us all guessing each day which streets we would be able to use. The digging, huge pieces of equipment, the re-tracking so the train could still run were all an unbelievable challenge in itself. Added to that were the many freeway re-dos, sewer and water pipe repairs, and general road repair, bringing us all to a panicked state whenever we saw those bright neon orange signs alerting to "ROAD WORK AHEAD."

God has roadwork to do on our journey with him. There will be times when that highway is smooth and clear, but what lies ahead? Generally, he has a great deal of major construction work to do in us. We always think of the Apostle Paul as someone who always had it all together, knowing exactly what to do and say. He stated many times in Scripture that he had not arrived, but that God was still working in him. "Not that I have already obtained *it*, or have already become perfect..." and "Brethren, I do not regard myself as having laid hold of *it* yet..." (Philippians 3:12-13), the *it* referring to conforming to the image of Christ. And that is God's goal for us, to make us more like Christ.

As I travel through town these days and am confronted with cones, signs, and detours, I am learning to ask God what area of my life needs repair, instead of allowing my blood pressure to rise over the inconvenience. Do I need major work in attitude adjustment? Is a re-track required to circumvent distractions that hinder my relationship with God? Am I taking a detour because I'm not trusting God to get me through the rough, rutted road ahead? I must surrender to the Master Road Builder and to whatever "road work" he has planned for me.

Prayer:

Father God, I need major work. I know you are far from finished with me. Do whatever you have to do to make me more like your Son. Amen.

Thought for the Week:

ROAD WORK AHEAD: COUNT ON IT!
What road work has God revealed that needs to be done in you? A minor repair or a complete re-do?

Monday

Tuesday

Wednesday

Thursday

Friday

Saturday

Sunday

POWER OF PRIDE
(OR BEFORE THE FALL)

Read: Proverbs 11:2, 16:18, 29:23

I will break down your pride of power; I will also make your sky
like iron and your earth like bronze.
(Leviticus 26:19)

IN A RECENT Scripture study, I found pride mentioned fifty-six times. In only about three of those references was it mentioned in a positive light. The bumper sticker that appeared after 9/11, "Power of Pride" is exactly the downfall of many people and nations in Bible history. In Ezekiel 24:21 we hear the prophecy, "Speak to the house of Israel, Thus says the Lord God, 'Behold, I am about to profane My sanctuary, the pride of your power, the desire of your eyes and the delight of your soul; and your sons and your daughters whom you have left behind will fall by the sword.'"

Ezekiel 30:6, 18 and 33:28 also speaks of the pride of power that ends in destruction. In Isaiah 2:17, "The pride of man will be humbled, and the loftiness of men will be abased, and the Lord alone will be exalted in that day." Isn't our pride in ourselves as a country and our arrogance stating to the world, "We're better than you" one of the reasons for 9/11?

As for me, I know pride in my heart has been the reason for many falls. I can remember an incident in teaching a music appreciation class to eighty freshmen. I prided myself in that I had control of the class and did not resort to yelling as one of my colleagues felt he needed to do. He had the same number of students. But then came time for me to teach a music theory class for the first time. This class was much smaller and made up mostly of very undisciplined freshmen. Guess what? I yelled a few times! I have also noticed pride creeping into our conversations when we relate how busy we are, as if maxing ourselves out is something to be proud of.

A more serious occurrence is when pride slips into self-righteousness and I have exalted myself above others, priding myself that I have made better decisions or life choices. I am then no different from the Pharisee who thanked God he was not like other people. (Luke 18:11)

Churches also fall into the sin of pride by patting themselves on the back for their size, programs, out-reach, music, pastors, etc. The story of Nebuchadnezzar, the king of Babylon, is a good reminder. "The king reflected and said, 'Is this not Babylon the great, which I myself have built as a royal residence by the might of my power and for the glory of my majesty'" (Daniel 4:30)? No sooner were the words out of his mouth when Daniel delivered the prophecy that sovereignty would be taken away, he would be driven away from mankind, live in the fields, and eat grass like the cattle. It immediately came to pass (Daniel 4:28-37).

Pride is the downfall of us all. There are many stories throughout history of the pride of individuals and nations that have brought and continue to bring us all down in the insignificant as well as the monumental. The only power of pride is what we possess through the Holy Spirit as children of God.

Prayer:

Father God, please bring to my consciousness every time the sin of negative pride creeps into my mind, actions or words. May my pride be in you and in ways in which I can bring you glory. Amen.

Thought for the Week:

Pride really does go before a fall.
Each day this week, record an attitude of pride either in thought, word, or deed.

Monday

Tuesday

Wednesday

Thursday

Friday

Saturday

Sunday

GOD'S WORD

BOOKS

Read: Hebrews 4:12

All Scripture is inspired by God and profitable for teaching, for reproof, for correction, for training in righteousness; so that the man of God may be adequate, equipped for every good work.
(2 Timothy 3:16-17)

DO YOU HAVE a favorite novel that you have read numerous times? What is it? Maybe you have more than one, including a few battered favorites from childhood. I have one that is an old, yellowed paperback held together with a rubber band. I have read it more times than I can count, and each time it speaks to me in a different way when I read it. I first read it when in my twenties. The main character is fifty and the time period is after World War II. At the time, I just couldn't see how I was going to enjoy this book. I was twenty-one and couldn't fathom how a fifty-year-old could be a heroine! But it was one of those stories that held me and has continued to hold me over and over again, as I read about a quiet English village full of ordinary people. Now I'm on the other side of fifty and still learning from that book and those characters. There are even times when I am drawn to read it again to experience the wisdom and healing in its pages.

It is both interesting and revealing to reflect on novels read and how one becomes intimately involved with well-developed characters. One of those characters comes to mind and you wonder what they are doing now, only to be reminded that this person was in a novel you read!

Autobiographies and biographies continue to amaze and inspire as lives unfold and capture our hearts and minds. Teaching books by the giants of the faith, past and present, can be life changing for all of us as they share God's work through the successes and failures of their lives. Historical novels, my favorite, take us to another time and place, giving us a glimpse of what it might have been like to live in that era.

The book of books, the Holy Bible, is the ultimate teacher as God speaks to us through his Word. It contains so much that teaches us through biographies of Old and New Testament characters, wars, rebellions, love stories, poetry, proverbs, and all of God's instruction for living. Ultimately, it reveals who God is, his character, and his love for us revealed in Jesus Christ. So why don't we savor it as we do our favorite books?

Prayer:

Father God, when I read your book, teach me more about you. I want to become more intimately acquainted with you. Amen.

Thought for the Week:

The contents of every book had its beginning in God's Book!

Each day this week, recall a novel you have read wherein the plot, characters, and life lessons compare to those in the Bible.

Monday

Tuesday

Wednesday

Thursday

Friday

Saturday

Sunday

OPEN THE BOOK!

Read: 2 Timothy 3:16

David inquired of the Lord, saying, "Shall I pursue this band? Shall I overtake them?"
And He said to him, "Pursue, for you shall surely overtake them,
and you shall surely rescue all."
(1 Samuel 30:8)

DAVID, IN HIS many ups and downs as a "man after God's own heart," learned to "inquire of the Lord" in circumstances when he did not know what to do. In 1 and 2 Samuel, he sought the Lord many times asking if he should go up against the Philistines and how it was to be done. God answered and guided. In those times of depression, David cried out to the Lord asking why his soul was in despair. As he penned Psalms 42 and 43, David cried, "Why are you in despair, O my soul? And why have you become disturbed within me? Hope in God, for I shall yet praise Him, the help of my countenance, and my God." God answered him saying that he had to only hope in him, the help of his countenance.

Why is it I don't see, understand, or grasp what God says to me in every situation?

There are times when I am at the bottom of the pit that David mentions frequently in the Psalms. When I need, in desperation, that word, advice, place of help, I don't inquire of the Lord, as David did. Instead, I look in all the wrong places, namely, whatever the world has to offer in my circumstance. I know there is no answer there for anything, but I still pursue worldly wisdom, which is always a dead end. This wisdom of the age is that I am supposed to find the answer to everything within myself.

In reading Psalm 16:11, for example, the word is very clear. God says, "I have made known to you the path of life; in *My* presence is fullness of joy: in *My* right hand there are pleasures forever." Still I don't go where I need to go—to him, to his life giving word.

In other words, I don't *open the book*!

How can I use the Word as a lamp to guide my feet and light to my path, (Ps 119:105); and the Word as a sword, (Heb. 4:12); and the Word to teach, correct, reproof, train in righteousness, (2 Timothy 3:16), and hear (read) the Word to grow in faith, if I don't abide in his Words (John 8:31)? I have more than David had. I have the whole *book*. The Manufacturer's Handbook is written by the one who created me and desires a relationship with me. Everything I need for all of life is in there.

Prayer:

Father God, forgive me for not inquiring of you for everything. I have your living Word in my hands. As I open your Word, open my heart to receive more of you and your will for my life. Amen.

Thought for the Week:

Open the book!
Each day read one of the five Scriptures listed above.

Monday

Tuesday

Wednesday

Thursday

Friday

Saturday:
Which one spoke to you specifically?

Sunday:
Cross reference John 8:31.

SOURCES

Carmichael, Amy, From the book IF, by Amy Carmichael, Copyright 1938 by The Donhnavur Fellowship and published by CLC Publications, Fort Washington, PA. All rights reserved. Pg 15.

Chambers, Oswald, Taken from *My Utmost for His Highest,* edited by James Reimann, © 1992 by Oswald Chambers Publication Assn., Ltd., and used by permission of Discovery House Publishers, Grand Rapids MI 49501. All rights reserved. Quotes from days 4/25, 11/27, 11/23, 8/27, 12/24.

Evans, W. Glyn, *Daily With the King,* (The Moody Bible Institute of Chicago 1979) Used by permission. 1/14.

Hayes, Helen, American, actress, "When you rest, you rust." (GreatQuotes.com)

Goudge, Elizabeth, *The Scent of Water,* Copyright 1963 by Elizabeth Goudge Coward-McCann, Inc. New York. First American Edition 1963 pg 40-41, 166.

Livingstone, David, Quote from *Experiencing God* by Henry T. Blackaby & Claude V. King (Lifeway Press 1999) pg 135.

Lowry, Robert, (1826-1899) "Nothing But the Blood" hymn.

Pollard, Adelaide A., "Have Thine Own Way, Lord" hymn 1907.

Shoemaker, Sammuel M., *We Believe in Prayer* (T. S. Dennison & Company 1958) Quoted in *Stories of Prayer for a Healthy Soul* compiled by Christine M. Anderson, (Inspirto, the Gift Group of Zondervan 2000) pg 56. Used by permission of Zondervan.

Taylor, J. Hudson, Quote from *Hudson Taylor's Spiritual Secret* by Dr. & Mrs. Howard Taylor (China Inland Mission, Overseas Missionary Fellowship 1958) pg 107. Used by permission.

Warren, Richard, *The Purpose Driven Life* (Zondervan 2002) pg 117. Used by permission of Zondervan.

CONTACT INFORMATION

To order additional copies of this book, please visit
www.redemption-press.com.
Also available on Amazon.com and BarnesandNoble.com
Or by calling toll free 1-844-2REDEEM.

CPSIA information can be obtained
at www.ICGtesting.com
Printed in the USA
LVOW01s1639090117

520313LV00005B/468/P